SURVIVING IN SILENCE

SURVIVING IN SILENCE

A DEAF BOY IN THE HOLOCAUST

The Harry I. Dunai Story

Written by Eleanor C. Dunai

Foreword by John S. Schuchman

Gallaudet University Press   *Washington, D.C.*

Gallaudet University Press
Washington, DC 20002

Library of Congress Cataloging-in-Publication Data

Dunai, Eleanor C.
    Surviving in silence : a deaf boy in the Holocaust : the Harry Dunai story /
written by Eleanor C. Dunai ; foreword by John S. Schuchman.
        p. cm.
    Includes bibliographical references.
    ISBN 1-56368-119-6 (alk. paper)
     ISBN 978-1-56368-235-3 (paperback)
    1. Dunai, Harry, 1934– 2. Jewish children in the Holocaust—Biography. 3.
Jews—Hungary—Biography. 4. Holocaust, Jewish (1939–1945)—Hungary—
Personal narratives. 5. Holocaust survivors—Biography. I. Title: Harry Dunai
story. II. Title.

DS135.H93 D863 2002
940.53′18′092—dc21
[B]   2002066841
        ○
∞ The paper used in this publication meets the minimum requirements of
American National Standard for Information Sciences—Permanence of Paper
for Printed Library Materials, ANSI Z39.48-1984.

CONTENTS

FOREWORD
John S. Schuchman

IN BUDAPEST during the summer of 1997, I interviewed a dozen deaf
Hungarian Jews who had survived the Holocaust. A couple of the in-
terviewees mentioned that I should meet another Hungarian survivor who had emigrated to California. That survivor, Harry Dunai,
and I met the next summer. Fluent in both Hungarian and American
sign languages, he volunteered as an interpreter for the Gallaudet
University sponsored conference "Deaf People in Hitler's Europe,
1933–1945," which I and a colleague chaired. Subsequently, in August
1999 at his home, I interviewed Mr. Dunai about his own Holocaust
experiences. The next year, he accompanied a group of university
students, deaf and hearing, that I and a colleague led on a three-week
Holocaust tour of eastern Europe. The tour ended in Harry's former
home of Budapest where, in June 2000, we met with many other deaf
Jewish survivors.

Harry's memoir, the text of this book, is a unique story of survival. Born as Izráel Deutsch, the young boy survived the devastating
occupation of Budapest by the German army, the treatment of Jews
by the native fascist Arrow Cross organization, and the city's near
destruction by the victorious Soviet army in 1944 and 1945. Subsequently, he grew to manhood under the communist regimes where
the young deaf Jewish survivor changed his name to Imre Dunai,
found employment, and eventually convinced authorities to allow
him to travel to Sweden where he took advantage of opportunities to
emigrate to the United States.

Equally important, Dunai is a witness to the experience and importance that the Izraelita Siketnémák Országos Intezeté (Israelite
Deaf and Mute National Institute) on Mexikoí Boulevard provided
for deaf children and for the Budapest deaf community. The school

ix

building has survived the years and currently serves as a school for ambulatory and mentally disabled students. In the summer of 2000, we returned to this site, where our group of university students offered a prayer service in memory of the former deaf Jewish students. Afterwards, Harry shared his personal memories of the school with an audience of the current Jewish Deaf Association of Budapest.

As is the case with all personal narratives, it is useful to place the individual story in its historical context. The Jewish deaf residential school in Budapest was not unique. In the latter part of the nineteenth century, European Jewish communities created and supported four boarding schools for deaf Jewish children in Berlin, Budapest, London, and Vienna.[1] By the time that Nazi leader Adolf Hitler had ascended to power in 1933, the four schools possessed excellent reputations as progressive centers of oral education for deaf children and of Jewish education, which allowed some of the successful students to prepare for bar and bas mitzvahs. Although the London school survived until the mid-1960s, each school suffered during the war. After Kristallnacht in November 1938, Alex Reich, the superintendent of the Berlin School, accompanied a very small group of German deaf children to England, where they remained at the London school to await the outcome of the war. Most of their classmates who were left behind in Berlin were transported to the camps. The Berlin and Vienna schools never reopened, and the communist government closed the Budapest school a few years after war's end. Today, there are no residential schools in Europe for Jewish deaf children.

At the beginning of the twentieth century, sixteen boarding schools for deaf children were operating in Hungary. With financial support from philanthropists, the Jewish community created a school for the deaf in 1877 and a school for the blind in 1908. Shortly after World War I, the Pest Jewish Council merged those two schools into one, which was located at Mexikoí Boulevard in Budapest.

In his 1943–44 annual school report, the Mexikoí Boulevard school's director, Dr. Dezso Kanizsai, listed fifty-seven student boarders.[2] Izráel Deutsch (Harry Dunai) was listed as one of the students, and the annual report shows that he excelled in all of his studies at the highest level. When the German army occupied Hungary in the spring of 1944, the young boy was ten years old. The Germans immediately ordered most of the city's Jewish educational and charitable institutions to turn over their buildings. Along with other Jewish children, Deutsch shuffled from place to place until late January 1945 when the Soviet army liberated the city and thus enabled him, in the company of Director Kanizsai and other deaf children, to return to Mexikoí Boulevard. Some Holocaust scholars have referred to this period of ten to eleven months as a "whirlwind of destruction, resembling a genocide within the genocide."[3]

In this short period, more than a half million Hungarian Jews died.[4] It is ironic that during the previous four and a half years of war, the Budapest Jews suffered comparatively little in the face of the destruction of European Jewry all around them. As an ally of Germany in the first world war, Hungary lost two thirds of its territory in the peace agreement as a result of the Trianon Treaty at war's end. Enamored, however, with Germany's apparent economic and territorial successes with the rise of Hitler's Nazi regime in the 1930s, the Hungarian government, led by Regent Miklós Horthy and Prime Minister Gyula Gömbös, once again embraced alliances with the Germans. In the Vienna Awards, Hungary obtained territory from Czechoslovákia and Romania in 1938 and 1940, respectively, as a result of their German patrimony. In 1940, Hungary formally joined the Axis powers and the next year entered the war against Yugoslavia and the Soviet Union.

Hungary's estimated 900,000 Jewish population, particularly the approximately 200,000 Budapest residents, was one of the more assimilated Jewish communities in Europe. Historian Randolph L. Braham has referred to the period prior to World War II as a "golden era" for Hungarian Jews when they achieved both middle-class prominence and financial success in support of a Hungarian government dominated by a conservative aristocracy. Nevertheless, anti-Semitism was prevalent throughout Hungarian society. Several right-wing political organizations viewed the Jewish population as an internal social problem for Hungary. Throughout the 1920s and 1930s, Hungary imposed restrictive legislation on its Jewish population. In the mid-1930s, Hungarian fascists, led by Arrow Cross leader Ferenc Szálasi, gained popularity and were elected to numerous parliamentary seats. By the early 1940s, several thousand "foreign" Hungarian Jews had been deported and massacred. Despite these events, most Hungarian Jews remained safe. These were the years that young Dunai described as the happy and prosperous agrarian life of his family near the village of Komjata (formerly in Czechoslovákia, taken by Germany, and awarded to Hungary).

Near the end of the war in 1944, after the numerous defeats of their armies by the Soviets, the withdrawal of its Axis partner Italy from the war, and the imminent D-Day invasion of France by the Allied powers, the Hungarian government resisted Nazi demands for the Jewish population and sought to extricate itself from the war. Armed with knowledge of this threat, Hitler ordered the German army to occupy Hungary on March 19, 1944. Although Horthy retained his title as regent, government control remained in the hands of Germanophiles and, ultimately, was taken over in the fall by Hungarian fascists, the Arrow Cross.

Adolf Eichmann, the chief administrator for Jewish affairs, arrived immediately in Hungary and, with the help of the Hungarian bureaucracy, oversaw the deportation and transportation of Jews to the killing camps, primarily Auschwitz in Poland. By midsummer, Eichmann could report that the Hungarian countryside was rid of Jews. The government ordered the Budapest Jews to vacate their homes and to move to so-called "yellow star" houses to make room for the Hungarian Christians whose homes were now subject to allied bombing attacks. All Jews older than the age of sixteen served in forced-labor brigades under the supervision of the Hungarian military. Because Budapest Jews were made more visible by the "yellow star" markings on their residences and clothing, Arrow Cross militia and fascist thugs routinely robbed and brutalized them throughout these months. Various organizations such as the International Red Cross and individuals such as Swedish diplomat Raoul Wallenberg tried to help.

The Mexikoí Boulevard school's Director Kanizsai faced a terrible dilemma; should he send his students home to their parents or keep them together in Budapest?[5] When the Germans ordered the school to be turned over to for military use, the city's Jewish institutional directors decided to bring all of the children together to the Jewish Orphanage for Boys and Girls. Dr. Kanizsai decided that his blind students would not fare well if integrated with other children and sent them home to their parents. Some of the parents also demanded the return of their deaf children. However, neither Dr. Kanizsai nor the parents knew that groups outside the capital city of Budapest would be the first to face deportation and transport. Unfortunately, these two groups of children and their parents were the first from the school to be sent to the camps. Harry Dunai waited for word from his parents, but he never received any communication from them.

Eventually, the Mexikoí Boulevard school's buildings and its adjacent grounds became a center for the International Red Cross, where several thousand Jews sought refuge, including adult deaf Jews who were alumni of the school and familiar with its environs. In the late fall, the Arrow Cross attacked the center and sent adult Jews, including a group of deaf adults, to the Bergen-Belsen camp in Germany. Dr. Kanizsai kept the younger children, including Dunai, together, and they were forcibly moved to the ghetto adjacent to the Doheny Street Synagogue, where they remained until liberation by the Soviet Army on January 18, 1945.

At war's end, Dunai learned that, although some of his siblings survived, he now was an orphan. In the summer of 2000, we traveled to Auschwitz. During our tour of the camp and barracks in the company of young deaf and hearing university students, Harry found a commemorative list of Hungarians killed. There, he found the names of his parents and his eldest and youngest brothers. Afterwards, at the remains of one of the crematoria, Harry shared parts of his story with us. This book describes the story of his survival during and after the war. It is a remarkable story, and it represents the first major publication of a deaf Jewish survivor's memoir.

PREFACE

THREE YEARS ago, for the first time in my father's life, he told me about his childhood and his young adult life. And with this book, I have tried very hard to write all the facts of his memory while keeping his voice intact. Originally, I had written this biography in the third person as my father told me the events in his life from birth until 1963. But to allow the reader a more expressive and personal glimpse into his life, I have revised it and written it from his perspective.

There were, however, some barriers in accomplishing this. My father found it difficult, as would any Holocaust survivor, to express and share his emotions about his experiences. He also does not have a strong command of the English language. And, of course, his sign language follows a much different syntax than spoken English. Therefore, I interpreted his expressions, emotions, and words to convey the meaning I believed to be his intent.

I felt very privileged and honored to hear his story. As a result, I have been blessed with a part of history, and I believe he has come to terms with many of his demons.

ELEANOR C. DUNAI

ACKNOWLEDGMENTS

I AM TREMENDOUSLY grateful to my father for his openness in sharing his life story with me, and allowing me to take his voice and feelings by putting them into words. Because of this I have a deeper understanding of who he is today. He has also provided me with a deeper and different level of understanding of humanity, hatred, family values, religion, politics, and love that I may not have known.

Heartfelt gratitude goes to my cousin Steven Antin for his guidance and words of encouragement. His confidence in my ability to see this project through from beginning to end meant a lot. Great appreciation is given to my sisters Hannah Alfandari and Karen Tupuola for their listening ears, honest opinions, and good solid advice. I am also thankful to another cousin, Keith Ishida, for his input at the infancy stages of this manuscript.

I would also like to acknowledge Alan Adelson of the Jewish Heritage Press for reviewing the manuscript, and meeting with my father and I. Those several days of working as a team will forever be etched in my memory.

Innermost love is given to David and our two children, Zack and Ilona, for their support, patience, and positive feedback throughout this whole process. Finally, I feel fortunate to have family and friends who showed genuine interest and concern in this project.

SURVIVING IN SILENCE

IN THE BEGINNING

THE DATE was March 15, 1934, and I, Izráel Zachariah Deutsch, came into the world. I have no clue whether I was born in the morning, afternoon, or evening. I do know that I was born at our farm home, situated in the village of Velky Komjata, Czechoslovákia, located in the Carpathian Mountains region between the counties of Bereg and Ugocsa.

I was the ninth child in a family of ten children. My mother, Ilona Mermelstein, had dark hair and brown eyes. She was somewhat tall and small framed. She came from a wealthy family and was an industrious woman, taking care of the household, running the farm, and managing our home-based business. She was strict, yet was a loving and caring mother. She was also a good wife to my father, Mordechie Deutsch, or Mór, as he was called by his family and friends. My father had strawberry blonde hair and grayish-blue eyes. He was tall and slim, with broad shoulders. He was a learned man and most loving. I believe my parents were brought together from traditional matchmaking.

From what I recall and from what my siblings have shared with me, my mother essentially did everything. I saw my mother as the business-minded one when compared to my father. My father was an educated rabbi, receiving his master's degree in rabbinical studies, which prepared him to be a rabbinical judge known as a Dayan. He did not have his own congregation or act as a Dayan; however, he was the leader of our local Jewish community. Within our home, my father practiced all the laws of Judaism. I still remember how he wrapped the tefillin around his arm and how he rocked as he prayed. My father's father was a practicing rabbi in the town of Nitra. Unfortunately, I do not have a deeper knowledge of his status within his community. My father also worked as a merchant at our home-based business, which was a general store. The general store was located in the front room of our home and was separated simply by a wall.

My oldest brother was Miklós, who had dark brown hair and olive skin. My sister Jolán followed, with auburn hair, fair skin, and hazel eyes. Then came the twins—a sister, Hainsha, with dark hair and olive skin, and a brother, Salgo, with auburn hair, fair skin, and gray-blue eyes. Hainsha died when she was four years old from a bout with pneumonia. Then came three additional sisters—Lenke, with auburn hair, fair skin, and hazel eyes; followed by Magdalena (a.k.a. Magda), with dirty-blonde hair, fair skin, and hazel eyes; and then Irén, with dark brown hair, olive skin, and brown eyes. Sándor (a.k.a. Naftali, Tuli) was the eighth, with dirty-blonde hair, fair skin, and hazel eyes. I was the ninth, with dark brown hair, olive skin, and brown eyes. I was often called Chári, a shortened form of my middle name Zachariah. The tenth and last was my brother Jakab (a.k.a. Jenő) with dirty-blonde hair and fair skin.

Our home was beautiful, encompassing approximately 1,500 square feet, with plenty of attic and basement space. There weren't enough bedrooms for all of us, so my mother, father, Jenő, and I slept together in one bed in the kitchen. Once in a while, I'd sneak into bed with Irén and Magdalena because they gave me comfort and I adored them. The rest of the beds held two children each. The perimeter of the house was laden with red and green grapes, which we ate, crushed into juice, or fermented into wine that we stored in barrels in the basement. We also had enough fruit trees, plum and apple, to provide fruit for our family and fruit to sell in our general store. And my mother made the best plum jam in town.

We had acres and acres of farmland and grew a variety of crops, including corn, potatoes, squash, barley, alfalfa, wheat, and sugar beets. Sunflowers that we planted in a fence formation around the perimeters of the fields provided a source of food, protection, and privacy. Our water supply came from a well located at the back of our house. Our bathroom, an outhouse, was also located outside.

Some of the farm yields went to the mill, which was located approximately ten to fifteen minutes walking distance from the farm along a river. The mill was powered by the river water. When the squash and sunflower seeds were harvested, we took them by sack loads to the mill for processing. The sunflowers seeds were cooked and pressed into pancake-shaped molds, about twelve inches in diameter. The pressing of the sunflower seeds produced oil that later was used for cooking. My brothers and sisters and I loved nibbling and sucking on the sunflower seed pancakes, even though they were supposed to be saved for the cows. We fed the cows by breaking up each pancake into smaller pieces and mixing them with hot water, which my mother told me was so nutritious that the cows produced richer milk. The wheat, barley, and corn also went to the mill to be ground into flour and meal that my mother and sisters used to make breads and cakes. The leftover wheat bran, barley, corn, potatoes, and alfalfa were mixed with water and used for animal feed.

Nothing was wasted. Even the wheat husks were used in several ways. My mother creatively stuffed our mattresses with the husks. However, the husks had a more important use, and I would watch as my older brothers and sisters fulfilled this particular barn chore. First, they spread out the husks on the barn floor so the animals could sleep on them. Later, after the animals had soiled the husks, they raked them into a pile and dumped them into a compost bin. The pile eventually decomposed into fertilizer that my siblings spread over the fields for the intended spring and summer crops.

Similarly, our many animals served multiple functions. Four tan and white cows provided milk that we drank and made into other dairy products. One specific cow also hauled the crops from the fields. Approximately ten lambs in a variety of black, cream, and white coats supplied wool that we made into fabric or used as stuffing. Flocks of geese, roosters, and chickens in a variety of colors supplied us with eggs in all sorts of shapes, colors, and sizes. The territorial geese were also a natural home security system, and their feathers made good stuffing for our pillows and blankets. We raised cats and kittens to rid the house and barn of unwanted rodents. Rodents could potentially spoil the animal feed, crops, and food supply. All of us children were responsible for taking care of the animals. If any animal fell ill, my mother called the veterinarian immediately. She didn't like to see them suffer.

Once in a while, a rabbi who was certified to slaughter animals according to the kosher dietary laws came to the farm. As he slaughtered a lamb, he cut it open and blew up its stomach. If a lamb had a hole in its stomach, we were forbidden to eat it. However, it wasn't wasted because we could sell the meat to other people who did not keep kosher. We would then have to select another lamb for slaughter until we found one that met the dietary law. Chickens and geese were also slaughtered for meat.

Overall, the farm was our livelihood. It gave us our food and also provided the necessary provisions to sell in the general store, including the harvested goods, various tools, and textiles.

We lived in a quaint village. The road to it was a single-lane route made of dirt and cobblestone. Off in the distance stood the grand Carpathian Mountains in a sea of forestry laced with beautiful flowing rivers. Homes encompassed acres of land, so very few families lived in the area.

All the neighbors seemed helpful to one another. Some were Jewish; some were not. In our village, religion didn't seem to determine friendship. My family, though modern, was religious, flawlessly kosher, maintaining separate dishes for our meat and dairy meals. During every Sabbath, from Friday evening through Saturday evening, a Greek Orthodox neighbor came to our home and took care of any necessary duties that our family could not do. For example, on Saturday mornings, we weren't allowed to light matches. In fact, we weren't allowed to do anything that was considered work. We weren't allowed to have money in our pockets. When we finished praying at the synagogue, we came straight home and ate our lunch. Our neighbor came over to perform any small chores such as lighting candles and left without a word mentioned. When it became dark, we were able to light the candles ourselves and follow through with our chores.

My sisters did not receive religious training, but they learned the kosher dietary laws and how to observe the holidays. My brothers, however, were trained to pray; my father expected them to follow in his footsteps. My father took my brothers into a separate room to perform his teachings. Of all my brothers, Salgo was the only one I did not see in training. Salgo was the "worker." He normally left the house at 3:00 or 4:00 A.M. to do the farm work, so I didn't see much of him.

My father did not teach me how to pray because I was different from the rest of my siblings; however, my father rocked and comforted me on Sabbath evenings, times that were full of love. For reasons we still don't fully understand, my world fell silent when I was about a year old. One of my sisters told me that Lenke had left me unattended on the living room table for only a minute while she ran into the kitchen to tend to something. Lenke returned to the living room where she found me lying on the clay tile floor. In a panic, my mother called the local town doctor to check on me. The doctor's diagnosis was a minor bump to the head, and he advised her not to worry.

How my deafness occurred was and still is not important because I have lived out my life, surviving in silence. Although I no longer heard the geese screeching, kittens meowing, lambs baaing, children screaming, or my father davening, nobody knew at the time of my hearing loss. My world and life within it seemed to go on as usual. As time passed, however, my siblings began complaining to our parents that I was ignoring them, not listening to them, or not responding to their questions. Like many parents, my parents brushed off the subject and attributed my behavior to laziness. Not until later did they notice that I did not react to sound.

My father believed that I was all right. I remember my father having me sit on his lap for hours while he read the Bible to me. Trying to keep me entertained, he allowed me to meddle with his gold pocket watch. He never noticed that I didn't bother to listen for the ticking sound that a watch could make. But after my mother observed my behavior over a long period, she finally realized that something didn't seem right.

When I was two, my mother wrote letters to various doctors throughout Europe. A Swedish doctor came to our home to give my parents an accurate diagnosis of my condition. The doctor concluded that I was deaf and mute. He suggested to my parents that an operation be performed and felt the chance of success was high. My mother felt that I was too young and wanted to wait until I turned five or six years old.

In the interim, my family and the community used body language to communicate with me. They pointed to me and then to their own mouths, which meant they wanted me to eat. And if I pointed to my food and then to my mouth with an ugly face, they understood that I didn't like the food. If I pinched my nose and pointed to my food, my family knew I didn't like the smell. When they pointed to me then rubbed their own stomachs, I knew they wanted me to go to the bathroom. If they put their hands together to one side of their faces, I knew I had to go to bed. Finally, if they gently rubbed my arm, I knew I was being a good boy. My family treated me with a great deal of love, and I knew I was part of the family. Being an enthusiastic child, I was always alert and ready to be a part of what was happening. Everyone fussed over me, yet I was treated no differently when it came to doing my share of the chores. I worked alongside my brothers and sisters on our farm.

CHAPTER **2** (1938–1940)

MISCHIEVOUS CHILDHOOD AND DARKENING POLITICAL CLOUDS

BEFORE WORLD WAR I, Slovakia, the eastern region of Czecho-slovákia where I grew up, had been part of the Austro-Hungarian Empire and gained its independence after that war. Politics began to take a dramatic shift in 1938. During that year, Germany took over Czechoslovákia. Also during this time, Hitler labeled all Slovaks and Gypsies as subhuman and Jews as nonhuman.[1] Hitler had become a full-fledged fascist dictator in Germany. Hungary also had its own soon-to-be dictator, Ferenc Szálasi. Szálasi was known as the creator of "Hungarianism." Hungarianism was a philosophy that incorpo-rated Magyar nationalism with German National-Socialist (Nazi) principles.

Amid these darkening political clouds, I viewed my home life as idyllic. However, even though I was too young to be aware of the potential of my future, my father believed that the farm life would never afford me a whole and peaceful life. He decided that, for me to have a future, I would need an education. Besides, some of the vil-lage children, knowing I was deaf, mocked me with hand signals, teased me, or tried to hurt me. I would complain to Sándor, who in turn, would find the culprit or culprits and beat them up. Sándor was my best brother—my protector. I believe my parents knew that I would suffer from discrimination because of my deafness. Possibly, they knew or had heard rumors of the sterilizations going on in Nazi Germany.[2]

My parents considered a government-run school for the deaf in the city of Ungvar (now named Uzhgorod), sixty miles to the north of our village. My parents knew of this place because another deaf boy from our village attended the school. His father worked for the post office. I could never figure out why the postman liked me so

7

much. He was always smiling and nice to me, and I was nice back to
him. Years later, my brother Salgo told me that the postman had
a deaf son. Eventually, my parents decided against the government
school because they believed the government and the general political climate was anti-Semitic. In addition, kosher laws were not kept
at the school. Instead, my parents decided that a Jewish school located in Budapest would be the best solution.

By the early months of 1939, Szálasi's Hungarian followers
founded the Arrow Cross Party, also known as the Hungarist Movement.[3] His followers were from the earlier Party of National Will,
founded in 1937, which ended up being banned by the government.
This Arrow Cross Party and the National Socialist Hungarian Party
were now the far-right groups in Hungary.

In Germany, Hitler officially declared his xenophobic views. He
favored the idea of a single race, fearing those who were different. He
was an advocate of eugenics. Even as far back as 1933, before Hitler
grew powerful, the German Ministry of Justice had proposed death
for those who were considered defective and biologically inferior,
including people who were deaf.[4] Sterilization was the substitute
for blatantly ridding the world of this inferior population. I don't
remember where I learned about the final figures, but I believe approximately 375,000 people were sterilized. Judges, mental health
practitioners, and health workers were involved in the sterilizations
and, later, in the killings.[5] I learned recently that sterilizations had
been going on since the nineteenth century. At the end of the nineteenth century, the first notions of genes and heredity were coming
from Mendel and Darwin, and those ideas very quickly lent fuel to
social prejudice. It became a great stigma for a family if one of their
children married someone in a family that had mental illness, deafness, or any other problem that might be attributed to genetics.
In fact, I was shocked to learn that the United States conducted sterilizations, too.

During the summer of 1939, I was busy being quite the mischievous child. My deafness did not prevent me from being an explorer.
I had total freedom, was considered spoiled, and rarely received any

form of punishment. However, one outburst brought me harsh consequences. On one occasion when I got angry, I threw a rock at the window on the kitchen door, breaking the glass. My father took the belt and whipped me. I cried. After that, I was very quiet. Magdalena told him that I was sorry, and she comforted me. That was the first and last time he ever whipped me with the belt. I think he felt guilty.

I had many other adventures that should have landed me a severe punishment. One day, a neighbor boy and I decided to play with matches. We struck a match, placing it at the base of the hay house, which was located near the barn. We did not realize we would be setting the hay house ablaze. The house was stacked high with wheat husks.

In just seconds, we noticed both our families and neighbors running from all directions toward us. I turned around and saw the hay house ablaze. I realized that my friend and I had done something wrong. I ran over to the fire and could feel the scorching heat on my body. The flames completely engulfed the hay house and began threatening the barn. Everyone ran wildly, trying to put out the flames. Each bucket of water had to be hand cranked from the well and passed from person to person, an extremely slow-moving task. Fortunately, the fire was doused, and the barn was spared. Afterwards, my parents wanted to know how the fire got started in the first place. I think it was my neighbor friend who told. Amazingly, I was never chastised for the incident. I guess they figured I just didn't understand. I was just a child. The matches were there and so it wasn't my fault. My parents were obviously remarkable and very forgiving.

My explorations continued, and once again, I innocently encountered danger. Sometime during the summer, I ventured out into the fields and explored the farm buildings, unaware that my mother had been looking for me for some time. Finally, she spotted me at one of the farm buildings. I was filthy from head to toe. My mother was upset and swatted me with a wooden switch. After that, I did not disappear again, although I continued to explore.

Later, I discovered a bag of poppy seeds and decided to eat them. I found some bread and brushed sunflower oil on it. Then, sprinkling a mound of poppy seeds over the bread, I ate my creation. The seeds took their narcotic effect, and of course, I fell asleep. Many hours later, I awoke to Jolán slapping me on the face. She asked, "What is wrong with you?" I told her what I had eaten. She wagged her index finger at me while I read her lips. "Nem," she scolded, which meant "no." My entire family regularly told me no without explanation because communication was so difficult. Looking back, I am sure they were equally frustrated with me as I was with them.

As summer came to an end, my mother and I prepared for our journey to the "Pest" side of what is now Budapest. Before World War I, Buda was inhabited primarily by people of German descent, and Pest was inhabited primarily by people of Hungarian descent. Buda was the city with the hills whereas Pest was the flat city. Mother wanted to make sure I arrived at the deaf school on time for the fall semester to begin. As we were leaving, everyone had tears in their eyes. I couldn't figure out why everyone was crying and making a big fuss over me. I was completely unaware of my family's intentions to leave me at a residential deaf school in Budapest. They did not explain the purpose of the trip. I was traveling, following along; I knew nothing.

The train ride to Budapest covered several hundred miles. Two deaf schools were located there—one that was run by the government and one that was a Jewish school called the Izraelita Siket-némák Országos Intezéte (Israelite Deaf and Mute National Institute). My mother's plan was to visit the institute. When we arrived, we met Dr. Deszo Kanizsai, the principal of the school. He was a tall man with a hefty, well-developed body and a few red streaks running through his pure white hair. He lived at the school along with the children. He was Jewish as were most of the counselors and teachers.

Dr. Kanizsai gave us a partial tour of the institute. We saw the hallway, foyer, office, dining room, and one classroom. Then, we went into Dr. Kanizsai's private office, and my mother talked with Dr. Kanizsai. I was bored and went out to watch the other children in one of the classrooms. Then, I saw my mother and Dr. Kanizsai walk out into the hallway. My mother was quiet. She shook Dr. Kanizsai's hand good-bye.

Mother had been unaware of the age requirement for attendance, which was six years old. I was only five, which meant she had to take me back home. I wasn't disappointed because I had no idea why we were visiting the school in the first place. When my mother arrived home with me still in tow, my family was surprised and delighted. Life quickly got back to normal. I was once again the mischievous explorer. The following year, however, I would return to the school.

On September 1, 1939, Germany invaded Poland. World War II was advancing full steam ahead. At this time, Hungary didn't want any part of the war. Prime Minister Teleki declared Hungary a non-belligerent nation after the German invasion of Poland.[6] Standing by this declaration, Teleki opened the border with Poland, granting approximately 150,000 fleeing Poles political asylum. But Teleki felt tension in maintaining independence from Germany. Hungary had been supplying the Germans with raw materials such as oil and iron as well as farm goods while refusing to commit any Hungarian troops to Germany's cause.[7] Teleki made clear that the reason he was supplying the materials was that he wanted Hungary to get back all of its Slovak territories that it had lost in World War I.[8] Teleki was successful with the land deal, and my hometown of Velky Komjata changed its name to Magyar Komjat, or Komjat for short.

In the meantime, Teleki privately assured the British that Hungary was not completely on the side of the Germans. Unfortunately, Teleki was not able to convince the many Hungarians who wanted to be a part of the success that the other countries seemed to be achieving with Germany at the forefront. Szálasi's Arrow Cross movement grew, robing the Arrow Cross militants in uniforms with black boots and green shirts.

By now, sterilization was no longer an option for the so-called unhealthy undesirables. The sterilization idea had been designed to prevent undesirable offspring. However, Germany still found the unhealthy undesirables an economic disaster and, instead, created the action for euthanasia.[9] The program was developed to cleanse the race of undesirable blood. To further matters, in October 1939, physicians began filling out forms detailing the victims—their patients—and listing their races. The path was now open for killing Jews, Gypsies, and defective undesirables, regardless of their health status. Six special killing centers were set up in Germany. The first victims to receive the fatal injections were babies and children. Parents were told that their babies and children were sick and needed to be cured and that they would be sent to special wards where the parents could not have contact.

In addition, Hitler approved the killing of institutionalized adults. Naturally, the judiciary cooperated because it believed that Nazi medical science and policy was necessary to solve the problem of the sick and "criminal" Jews. In addition, part of the medical policy was to loot the deceased bodies, retrieving gold to be recycled and human organs to be used in the name of medical research.

CHAPTER **3** (1940–1941)

THE INSTITUTE

A YEAR HAD passed and it was fall again, September 1940, to be exact. I was excited that I could visit Budapest again. However, I was still unaware of the real purpose of our trip. The communication between my family and me was still limited to body language. My voice conveyed only grunts, groans, moans, screeches, and laughter. My knowledge was acquired strictly from observation. I was able neither to express my full thoughts nor to ask any detailed questions, specifically, the reason for our trip back to Budapest. Yet, I was curious. My mother was packing a tiny suitcase with a couple sets of my shirts and pants.

The train ride to Budapest was wonderful. Any trip away from the farm was exciting. From the train station, we took a trolley to the institute. When we arrived, I recalled my visit to the institute from the prior year. The red-brick building stood out in an empty field. Dr. Kanizsai was there to greet us as we entered the building through the heavy, hardwood entrance doors. We immediately began our full tour. The walls in the building were very thick. All the floors were made from concrete and were quite smooth. Each room had stand-up heaters and double-paned, French-style windows with no curtains. By 1942, these windows would be covered each night by a wood frame enclosing black paper to fulfill blackout requirements during the war.

The basement of the institute was a bomb shelter and a storage area for coal and wood. The ground floor contained the dining room, grand hallway, gymnasium, and machine shop. The first floor held the offices, classrooms, and social room. I was surprised to see a piano in the social room. It was for five blind students (three boys and two girls) who also attended the institute. However, the social room was primarily used for students to complete homework assignments, converse, and play chess. The second floor had more class-rooms, the girls' dormitory, and Dr. Kanizsai's home at the end of the hallway. In front of the girls' dorm room stood the nurse's room and a room for the counselors. The third floor was the boys' dormitory and the laundry room.

After the tour, my mother and Dr. Kanizsai stepped into his office. They told me to sit out in the hallway while they spoke in private. I peeked in at one point and could see they were having an intense conversation. I noticed that my suitcase was no longer in the hallway. My mother came out of the office. She rubbed her stomach, which meant she needed to go to the bathroom. She told me to wait. What I didn't know was that Dr. Kanizsai had suggested she leave me in the corridor and then wait in his office.

As soon as she walked away, one of the counselors motioned for me to come into his classroom, which was filled with children. I refused, indicating that I was waiting for my mother. The counselor again motioned for me to follow him. Again, I refused. He came toward me and gently grabbed a hold of my wrist, pulling me into the room with the other children. I had no voice to say no or to speak up for myself. I fought with the counselor, and he failed to get me into the classroom. Finally, a couple of counselors grabbed me and pulled me into a dorm room. I was screaming with a lion's voice. I could not scream words because I didn't know any. For more than an hour, I screamed like a lion. The principal was one floor below me. Apparently, he couldn't stand hearing my outcries. He came up to the dorm and grabbed me. He shook me, placing me firmly on the ground and telling me, "Shush! Shush!" He never smacked me, but as I continued to scream, he kept at me until I finally calmed down. Then, the nurse came and gave me some pajamas. I was very upset and cried myself to sleep.

The next day, everybody went to class and I refused to follow. I was quiet and depressed. I wondered about what had happened to my mother. I felt abandoned. I didn't eat, drink, or try to communicate for about two days. Sári néni Balkányi, one of the teachers, came to my room and tried to comfort me. To this day, I feel a tremendous amount of sadness about the separation from my mother, and it still brings tears to my eyes. I had no idea that Dr. Kanizsai was the one who thought it best for her not to say good-bye. He believed that her saying good-bye would upset me. Not until October 1997 did I find out from one of my sisters that my mother had gone into the principal's office according to his instructions. She felt guilty leaving me behind, not saying good-bye. She sat in his office crying as she heard me screaming and wailing.

For the next couple of days, I was fearful. I refused to get out of the bed because I had both wet and soiled my bed. The nurse came and cleaned me up. I was so afraid. Sári néni came back and tried to comfort me, telling me not to worry.

I waited and waited for my mother, but she did not return. My heart was broken. My brain churned with questions that went unanswered. I felt lost without my brother and sisters. Everybody was a stranger.

Dr. Kanizsai and the counselors accepted my rebellious attitude by allowing me to isolate myself. And, after a few days went by, I started feeling lonely. The barber came and cut my hair military style and shaved off my peyos, or sidecurls. I worried about what my father would say in response, and I was afraid that he would be angry with me when I got home. But the haircut was not my doing. The institute had a policy of cleanliness, especially because of lice; the barber was always called in when somebody needed a haircut. Some of the adults had hair, but that was by permission only. Besides, who would have helped me brush my hair? We were children living in a dorm.

After those first miserable and lonely couple of days, I decided to go to class. As I entered the classroom, I saw my teacher, Sári néni Balkányi. She was hearing as were all the teachers at the institute. Sári néni was young and attractive. She had wavy, short, dirty-blonde hair and smiling hazel eyes that sparkled from behind glasses. About five feet, three inches tall and slender, she dressed like a lady. Sári néni introduced me to the class, and I was welcomed and accepted by the other children. I recall recognizing a strange feeling at that moment:

I was deaf. I began to feel a bit better. My transition would be a slow and gradual shift because I had never socialized with other children my age, especially deaf children, and I was extremely shy around them. I wasn't forward in this environment as I had been on the farm, and I had to learn some new skills.

During the months that followed, I began learning how to utter different sounds. Sári néni worked very hard, teaching me how to vocalize the consonants and vowels of the alphabet. She placed different-sized tongue depressors into my mouth and placed my own hand on my neck to feel the sounds I was making. Both techniques helped me to enunciate each letter of the alphabet correctly. Eventually, she taught me all forty-four letters of the Hungarian alphabet by helping me to master each one in order. Certain letters were easier than others. For example, the letter *b* required voicing from the throat whereas *p* was made from the lips only. The letter *e* had two different pronunciations, long and short, as did the letter *a*. The letters *o* and *u* each had four sounds. Sári néni put chalk powder in the palm of her hand and had me say the various vowel sounds in front of her palm so I could see the effect of the various pronunciations. The letter *k* was tricky. Sári néni took a water bottle and squirted it on the back of my throat, making me cough. As soon as I started coughing, she said, "This is *k*." Whenever I mastered a new letter, she gave me candy as a bonus.

None of us were taught sign language. Everybody was taught orally. But we all knew sign language, acquiring it naturally. During class time, we were forbidden to sign. We had to read one another's lips. When class time ended, we were free to sign. Everybody had a slight variation to his or her signing, but with the use of speech and speechreading in addition to our signs, we understood one another.

In November, my mother came back to the school to pay me a surprise visit. Apparently, Dr. Kanizsai had headed her off at the entrance. Even though he was an excellent teacher and principal, he was very strict. He strongly suggested that she not see me because he believed it would ruin any progress that I had made. However, he allowed her to peek in at me during my lesson.

Although she could not be with me or hold me in her arms, I guess she could see that I was being treated well. She left a basket filled with different fruits, various household items, and plum jam—enough for all the children. Then she left to visit other family members in Budapest. Dr. Kanizsai presented me with the basket later in the day, and I knew immediately that my mother had been at the school. I was silent at first, then began to cry, wondering why she wouldn't see me. Looking back now, I now realize that seeing her indeed may have made me feel worse.

In the meantime, the political front didn't look good. On November 20, Prime Minister Teleki lost his authority. Hungary had joined the anti-Soviet Axis alliance by signing the Tripartite Pact, which was the alliance of Germany, Italy, and Japan.[1] Although Hungary signed this pact, it also signed a friendship pact with Yugoslavia, fully knowing that Germany planned to take over Yugoslavia.

School had become a normal routine despite the political dramas. Each Friday, the nurse cut everyone's toenails, and all the children were required to shower. It was something we all endured. The youngest children went first, and the older ones were next. Then the adults held a prayer service followed by dinner consisting of whitefish and fish soup. In class, I began learning words containing the consonants and vowels that I could now vocalize. The first word I learned was *pá*, which means "good-bye." The second was *fa*, which means "tree." Naturally, *papa* and *mama* followed.

Despite my sadness for having to live at the school, I believed that, if I were a good student and did well, my mother would return for me. And I did do well. I also made friends. My first friend was Péter Faragó. Our mothers had communicated with each other and had established a relationship, which must have helped me connect with Péter. Péter had blonde hair and fair skin. He was trained well because his mother was a teacher. Márkus Kohn, a stout boy with brown hair and eyes, was another of my first friends. He looked like Hardy of the movie team, Laurel and Hardy. My mother knew his parents, and we had visited with them when I was about five years old. Márkus also had an older deaf brother. Both he and his brother were well trained. Péter and Márkus knew what they were doing, but I truly believed I was stupid and knew nothing. I was out of it. I looked up to them, and they were warm to me, helping me out. We all got straight As and competed with one another in every academic activity. I was very proud of myself. After grouping with Péter and Márkus, I eventually became friends with everybody.

Winter arrived, and I had to remain at the institute along with some other children. Some of the counselors also remained behind. I wondered why I couldn't go home when some of the other children could. Even though it was winter break, I continued attending school on a regular basis and continued with my speech lessons. My counselors decided that the break period was a good time to teach me some table manners.

Being deaf, I could not hear the inappropriate sounds I made, for example, slurping when I ate soup. The counselors taught me how to put the spoon in my mouth from a forward position rather than from the side. As we practiced, they let me know when I was making a slurping sound. They also taught me not to hit the inside of the glass with the spoon when I stirred, which made clanking sounds. The rules of etiquette seemed so unimportant, such a waste of time, and utterly ridiculous because they were never an issue back home. I followed the rules anyway, fearing that, if I didn't, I wouldn't ever be able to see my family again.

Aside from the required lessons of my winter break, I had plenty of opportunities for playtime. Hanukkah was a happy time. I got a dreidel, and everybody seemed to give us presents. A Jewish organization donated toys. I was excited. Except for a ball and scooter, which were at home in Komjat, I had never owned toys in my life. Those gifts eased my longing for home, and I began to find peace with the separation.

Spring had come, and as Hungary expected, Germany invaded Yugoslavia. This time, Hungary knew it would have to open its country to Germany because Hitler was demanding passage. Prime Minister Teleki tried very hard to stand his ground on behalf of Hungary. Hitler couldn't understand Teleki's refusal because Hungary had been providing them with raw materials to keep the German force in power. Immediately after Teleki's denial to Hitler, Admiral Horthy, the regent of Hungary, stepped in, giving Hitler the political rights he desired. Teleki, unable to cope with his failure, committed suicide on the third of April, 1941.[2]

School was moving along step by step. I continued mastering the alphabet and voicing new words. I was able to say Sári's name. All of us called her Sári néni (auntie). Péter and Márkus also taught me various board games. We played physical games, too, including running and hide-and-go-seek. I remember being very happy and laughing with all my friends. None of us really fought. However, I still missed my family and my farm home. I couldn't understand why my brothers and sisters were able to stay home and work while I had to live away at school. Finally, Sári néni told me I would be going home in June. I was overcome with joy and doubled my efforts at school.

Time raced by, and June arrived. I could finally go home! My excitement was tremendous. I was nervous, too, because, for some unexplained reason, I had to make the journey home alone. I was only seven years old. Sári néni was extremely concerned. She wanted to make sure I would arrive at the correct destination. To ensure my safety, she made me an identification plate. She cut a piece of chalkboard into a small square and attached a chain to the top of it. Then, she wrote my full name and point of destination on the board. I slipped the chain over my head, wearing the identification plate on my chest.

The train ride home seemed to take a lifetime. My mind raced with thoughts of my family and the farm. I was excited that I was going home and was not scared whatsoever, even when I had to make a challenging train transfer. When the train stopped in Bereg-Szász (now named Bereg-Ovo), I had to transfer to a smaller train because the Carpathian Mountains demanded too much of the larger trains. Seeing my identification board, the conductor approached me and, taking me by the hand, walked me down a plank to where I would board the next train. Then he signaled me to wait. A short time later, the small train pulled up, and I saw the conductor signal me to get on board. Thanks to the conductor and to Sári néni's preparations, I safely began the last leg of my trip, which zigzagged through the mountains and took me home.

When the train stopped, I wasn't sure whether I was in the right place. As I looked out the window, I saw my father and Jolán. My heart began racing with excitement. Quickly, I grabbed my suitcase, and stepping off the train, I yelled, "Jó napot kivánok," which meant, "Have a nice day." I'll never forget the look of surprise on their faces when they heard me utter those words. We exchanged long and happy hugs, then set out on our six-kilometer walk home.

When we arrived home, my mother opened the door, and I immediately blurted out, "Pá, mama, papa!" The entire family was shocked that I could speak and some of them began to cry. I remember my father telling my mother that I had also yelled the words "Jó napot kivánok." My entire family began talking to me. They were all there, all except Miklós, who had gone to the University of Bratislava, which was located west of Hungary. I understood bits and pieces of what they said. My vocabulary would improve day by day during my time at home. Before I entered the institute, I had had no vocabulary. Tapping on a shoulder had been the only way for me to get someone's attention, and my family had relied on getting my attention in the same way.

After all my worry, father never said a word about my missing peyos. In fact, I immediately noticed that Salgo did not have his peyos either. However, Sándor and Jenő had them. I think the break with tradition was a sign of change in our family.

My communication with the family had improved so much that I learned why I had had to make the journey home alone. The Hungarian government had created an order that no longer permitted Jews to own or operate a place of business. As a result, my father had to shut down our general store. We no longer had an income from the store, and our family had only enough for basic necessities, not for travel.

Under the circumstances, we worked particularly hard to keep the farm intact. My parents prayed that the political situation would eventually improve. In this way, life went forward. The chores got done and the farm continued operating.

We worked earnestly during the harvest, with Salgo and Lenke working the hardest. Together, we cut down the wheat with only hand-held scythes. Then we bundled up what was cut and stacked the bales of wheat in a crisscross pattern. Once the stacks were mounded high, we brought a cart pulled by our cow onto the field so we could manually load the wheat. Our poor cow had to pull the heavily loaded cart from the field all the way back to the barn. Once at the barn, powered machinery separated the wheat husks from the seeds.

To my dismay, I discovered during this summer the mystery behind one particular farm chore that was done every so often. In the past, I had joined either Irén or Magdalena as she went to the creek and tossed a potato sack into the water. I never knew what was in the sack and couldn't figure out why anyone would do such a thing. But this summer, I was instructed to toss the sack into the creek. As I grabbed and lifted the sack, I felt movement. Curious, I peeked inside and immediately felt sick to my stomach. My sister told me not to look and to throw the sack into the creek. I knew I had no choice.

Later, I learned that my mother had selected which kittens to keep and had sentenced the remainder to be discarded by means of the potato sack. This culling of the kitten stock ensured a continuing line of healthy cats. A collection of healthy cats was vital to rid the farm of rodents, which were a problem, especially in the barn. Sometimes the pests would bite the animals, contaminate the feed, and get into the food supply.

Aside from the daily chores, I found time to play with the neighbor children and with the farm animals, which I also loved to tease. I rode the lambs and mimicked the geese, letting them chase me afterward. However, being unable to hear warnings, my play continued to pose somewhat of a danger for me. On one occasion, while playing on top of a haystack in one of the farm buildings, I was oblivious to everyone yelling at me to get down. Naturally, I couldn't hear them. As they had feared, I fell off onto the hard ground. When I looked up, Jolán was hovering over me like a mother hen asking, "Are you okay, are you okay?" On another occasion while exploring in the local village, I also did not hear people yelling at me, and I almost got run over by a horse.

Between the chores and the play, my father, being the strict man that he was, continued impressing his Judaic training on my brothers, particularly Sándor. I was allowed to observe, and during the training, my father would sit me on his lap. If Sándor didn't follow directions, my father would hit him on his fingers with a stick or pencil.

Summer lasted for two and one-half months. I knew I had to leave, but I didn't want to because a whole flock of goslings had been born that were so soft, fluffy, and yellow—just perfect for hours of play. Leaving the animals made me sad. I was sure the cows would miss me, too. Although I didn't want to leave, I realized that the school was teaching me many things and was making it possible for me to communicate with my family.

I was relieved when my mother told me she was planning to accompany me back to the institute. When we arrived, Péter's mother and my mother chatted. The two of them seemed to get along well, laughing in conversation. I was pleased because Péter was one of my closest classmates. It was much easier this time when my mother had to leave. This time, we were able to say good-bye to each other. I didn't even cry.

After my mother left, I was flooded with a feeling of comfort. I recognized that all the children were like me. We shared a commonality—a bond of deaf culture.

Dr. Kanizsai had been busy talking with the parents. He was easy to spot with his tall large frame, hazel eyes, red-streaked white hair, and very fair skin. He always wore the same three-piece suit with a white, striped shirt and a necktie. Later, I found out that he could speak, read, and write English and German and that he had a doctorate degree.

After the parents left, Dr. Kanizsai called everybody to stand at attention, his way of getting us under control. I think he liked the power. In fact, whenever he entered our classroom, we all had to jump up and stand at attention, but we never saluted him. On this day, while we stood at attention, he announced which classrooms we would be attending. I had been promoted to the first grade.

School seemed better because I had made more friends. The students in my class were Antal Brandek, Margit Diamant, Tamás Dick, Sándor Einhara, Péter Faragó, Berta Indig, Erzsi Kálnoki, Márkus Kohn, Adolf Krausz, and Hermann Zoldán. My other friends in different classes were Leó Wachtenheim, József Weissz, and later, Ernö Rosenblüth.

This school year, Sári néni began focusing her attention on having me complete the alphabet. For the letter *l*, she lifted my tongue. For *m* and *n*, she pressed on my nose. The letter *r* was the hardest to learn, taking me two days. Making that sound required me to place my tongue on my teeth, blow to vibrate the tongue and roll the *r*, and combine it with the short *n* sound, all at the same time. I had so much difficulty that Sári néni made me first flap my lips to get the rolling feeling and then practice the rolling action with my tongue. The *s* sounds weren't as hard, but they involved learning three different sounds—sh, ss, and sz—that I had to keep straight in my mind. Finally, for the letter *y*, I had to learn how to fold my tongue. Naturally, each letter sound that I accomplished brought a reward of candy. Once I accomplished making all the letter sounds, we worked on building vocabulary and learning about sentence structure.

I began to feel that the institute was my second home. However, I found two things displeasing. First were the strict time regiments for academia and for playtime. Second was the perception that some children were being treated better than others. I began to observe who got what and why.

After a couple of months, I realized that children who were from wealthy families slept in Dr. Kanizsai's quarters. I later learned that their parents didn't want their "high-class" children mingling with commoners such as myself. These children not only got the better sleeping quarters but also received higher quality food, service, and accommodations. For example, a snack for me would consist of milk and plain bread. The children of "royalty" would receive milk and bread with butter and jam. They were also treated more as family members than as students. I am sure that the parents of these children paid ten times the amount for tuition.

Nevertheless, I felt that I could put up with these challenges. Besides, I had Sári néni, who kept me under her wing.

CHAPTER 4 (1941–1943)

WAS GOD WATCHING?

WINTER ARRIVED quickly, and I knew that I would have to remain at school with the other children. I envied those children who were able to go home and be with their families. For the first time, I understood the meaning of being poor. I realized that I was poor and that all the children knew I was poor, too. I swallowed my pride and reminded myself that summer was just around the corner and that soon I would get the chance to go back home.

During my winter break, I noticed the counselors bickering more than what I considered to be normal. They constantly disagreed about the information that was being reported in the newspapers. The students who remained argued, too, particularly Péter Altman and Leó Wachtenheim. Péter supported the Germans and Leó supported the communists. I tried to find out more information from the counselors. Leó was furious as he read the headline, "What Do We Do with the Jews?" He took the newspaper, tore it up, and threw it down. Naturally, the commotion heightened my interest in politics, but counselors didn't take the time to explain what was going on.

Later, I learned that the controversy had become apparent on January 20, 1942, at the Wannsee Conference. Up until that point, discussions had been taking place about what to do with the Jews. The Wannsee Conference was the platform to launch the Final Solution.[1] The Final Solution detailed a plan wherein Jews were to be put to death without exception. The Nazis' vision embraced a Judenrein (Jew-clean) world. This vision required that all Jews be rounded up wherever they lived throughout Europe and then be sent by train to specially built extermination camps in Poland. By "Jews," the Nazis meant all Jews—males and females, babies, children, adults, and the elderly. The Nazis had already been secretly

25

exterminating any undesirables up to this point, including Jews, certain non-Jews, and Gypsies. But now, the Nazis were openly stating that the Jews were a problem. The Final Solution also called for death by poisonous gas.[2] The decision to use poisonous gas was made because gas allowed hundreds and thousands of people to be killed at a time. I didn't know then, but euthanasia had already become a part of every hospital's routine, so the foundation had been laid for the mass killings. The other part of the Final Solution involved collecting everything from the victims, including clothing, jewelry, gold tooth fillings, hair, and skin. Some of the materials would then be sold to support the German effort.

I sensed that the future would not be good for the Jewish people. I knew that everybody was against the Jews. However, though the political outlook was bleak and anti-Semitism grew, my life went on as usual. I was unable to fully absorb the gloom and doom that my counselors were discussing on a daily basis. Even if they had attempted to help me understand, I don't believe I could have processed the effect of the situation on my life. I was just a child. So in a twisted sort of way, my deafness and my ignorance allowed me to look positively toward the future.

The spring months seemed to flow at a snail's pace. I was now officially a welfare student. I had to wear a uniform donated by the Jewish community. I was sure that the other children looked on me as a poor boy. I certainly felt like a poor boy. But I had to accept it in silence even though I was hurt and felt bad. Many parents brought presents for their children; I got nothing because my parents lived so far away. Also, most of the children got to go home for Hanukkah and Passover. I couldn't. But, on the brighter side, those parents who brought chocolate always brought enough for everyone to have a piece.

Then, finally, it was summertime. Once again, I took the train home alone, but this time, I was unafraid. On the train ride home, a farmer offered me some bread and smoked bacon. I knew about God's laws and about keeping kosher. I had been taught not to eat certain things because they were bad for my stomach. I told the farmer, "I can't, I can't." The farmer said, "Come, come." I replied, "I can't. God may be watching me." He laughed. I couldn't understand why he was laughing. My curiosity became stronger. I knew the smoked bacon was taboo, but I ate it anyway. It was so delicious. After eating it, I began feeling extremely guilty. I wondered whether God had seen me eating the unkosher meat. I looked out the train window to see whether God was watching me. And though I didn't see God, I felt that He was upset with me. The guilt stayed with me for a very long time.

Jolán met me at the train station. When we arrived home, the family was happy to see me, though no special homecoming or party awaited me, just the normal, day-to-day existence.

The very next day, I went to check on the goslings, which had grown into full-sized geese. I ran excitedly toward them. Not recognizing me, they began honking and flapping toward me. I quickly turned and began running away. They caught up to me in a matter of seconds, biting and bruising me on the behind. I'm sure they thought I was an intruder.

The summer typically brought unpredictable weather conditions, and this summer was no exception. The rainstorms were the most memorable events. Out of nowhere came storms with crashing thunder, bolts of lightning, and flash flooding. They began with thunder that made the ground shake. Then, thick clouds quickly piled up, and bolts of lightning blazed down from the heavens to the earth. The farm fields flooded within minutes, becoming miniature lakes. After the storm, the water receded, running off swiftly beneath our house along a trench that was specially designed for this purpose.

When the rain had stopped and the water had abated, my sisters and I foraged the fields in search of mushrooms. The mushrooms sprang up everywhere throughout the fields. We picked every type of mushroom and brought them back to the house for my mother to sort. She separated the edible ones from the poisonous ones. The whole process was very adventurous.

Although my communication had improved, I was still unaware of the depth of the political trauma that surrounded my world. I couldn't argue about politics; I just sat back and absorbed the mood. My father subscribed to a newspaper called the *Magyar Nemzet* (the Hungarian National). Every evening after dinner, Jolán read the newspaper to the family. I felt left out, not knowing what was happening in the family conversation. I began bugging my brothers and sisters to tell me what Jolán was saying. Finally, Magdalena and Irén began offering me explanations. From then on, the two of them became my interpreters. They were the best choice out of all my siblings because they seemed to understand me the most. Our communication system involved speechreading plus body language.

The general store in our home was open for business again, however, not by my parents, even though it was a part of our home. A non-Jewish husband and wife from the village were now using it to sell their goods. Luckily enough, it wasn't a terrible situation. We were fortunate because the couple liked my family. They especially liked me and always gave me a treat.

The summer was an especially difficult one because my family and I worked extra hard to maintain the farm and our livelihood. We had very little cash on hand, so we all pitched in, making additional butter, cottage cheese, and sour cream to sell at the open-air market. Getting to the market required a thirteen-kilometer trek by foot. Hauling the goods wasn't easy, and I considered the whole process an arduous task.

As summer neared its end, I began to think about the train ride back to school and, by association, about the smoked bacon I had eaten previously on the train. My guilt was heightened by the fact that it had not been the only time I had eaten pork. A neighbor boy had invited me to play at his home on several occasions during the summer. When we had our fill of playtime, we went up into the rafters of his family's barn where they kept their meat supply. There, we filled up with smoked bacon and kolbash, which is a hard, dry sausage. It was so good and filling that I could never resist saying no. But the guilt inside me now was enormous, and I constantly wondered whether God was watching me.

Like many young Jewish children, I didn't understand the why behind the pork taboo. So a few days before heading back to the institute, I asked my mother why our family couldn't eat bacon or sausage. She had a surprised looked on her face. Without explaining, she spit on the ground, and that was the end of that. My interpretation of the spit was that pork was bad, but that fact was not enough reason to convince me that I couldn't eat it. In addition, I had never gotten ill from the pork nor had I known anyone else who had.

Summer finally ended. I had to make the trip back to Budapest on my own because our cash was low. However, even at my young age, I understood the situation financially and somewhat politically. A Hungarian Jewish welfare organization paid for my journey back to Budapest and for my tuition fees at the institute.

On the train, I began to think about the institute. I was excited to see my friends and was curious about what was on the menu for the coming week. Each week, starting with Monday, the chef created a new menu. Sometimes the menu would repeat itself. Holidays, festivals, and special events would always yield a different meal. Most of the foods were excellent, especially the spaghetti squash. The kohlrabi, however, was stringy and awful.

My return to the institute went smoothly. I was promoted to the second grade. My interest in politics had grown immensely, especially after involving myself in family discussions during the summer months at home. My goal was to stay abreast of the news during the school year. I figured it would allow me to participate in the family discussions when I went home for my next vacation.

My writing skills improved rapidly, and I was evolving into an excellent math student—so much so, that nobody was able to stump me with mathematical problems. Sári néni couldn't believe my ability to solve problems and tried to figure out how my brain calculated. My secret was that I didn't sit there and calculate the equations; I simply memorized them. All I needed was one or two explanations and I understood. For example, Sári néni would tell me that three times eight equals twenty-four, eight times eight equals sixty-four, and so on. Then, she would immediately repeat the equations, and I would give her the answers. I also had help from the older children who would drill me.

I had grown very comfortable with the institute, and every once in a while, I didn't pay attention or talked too much to the other children. At those times, Sári néni pulled me aside and ordered me to stand in the corner of the classroom. Sometimes, she told me to put my fingers together, and she whacked me with a pencil. Sometimes, she described how I interrupted her lecture and how sad she felt about my behavior, which made me feel guilty, and I would cry. Sári néni always knew what to say to influence me. She was like a psychologist. But I was never embarrassed because the other children received equal punishment.

My friends and I were busy during our free time. A play was planned for Purim for which we were all assigned roles. Someone was to play Queen Esther, some of the children were to act as dwarfs, and a few children got to act as though they had eaten a poison apple. It was great fun. In addition, my new winter interest was observing chess games, even though I didn't understand the rules. I watched my counselor, Árpád Rákos, play against the other students, and I wished that I could play. I also gravitated toward every political discussion that I could find. The counselors were very willing to explain and discuss everything openly with me. I primarily observed their conversations because I was still very young. Not until 1944 would I be able to read more politics and involve myself in the discussions.

Spring came and went, and by June 1943, I was homeward bound on the train. Once again, my sister Jolán met me at the train depot. When I arrived home, I could see that the conditions from my prior visit had gone unchanged. My family was still struggling.

From the day I was born, I had not known anyone's name in the family. At the institute, however, I had learned the names of all my friends. As soon as I had the opportunity to ask, I tapped Jolán on the shoulder and questioned, "What is your name?" She replied smiling, "I am Jolán." Then, Irén said, "I am Irén." The rest of the family told me their names, too. Some of their names I could not vocalize cor-

Back row, left to right: Antal Brandek, Andor____, Leó Wachtenheim, Andor Kaufman, Jozsef____, Péter Altman, Bernáth Weicker, unknown, unknown, Andor ____, Antal Reizner, György Eiland, Sándor Weicker, Tibor____. Front row, left to right, Jancsi____, Ernö Rosenblüth, Péter Faragó, Adolph Krausz, Márkus Kohn, Lászlo Heinzelmann, Izráel Deutsch, Kastner____, Tamás Dick, Sándor Katz, Hermann Zoldán.

Of the twenty-five students in this photo of the 1943 class at the institute, nine are dead. Leó Wachtenheim was shot and killed by Arrow Cross soldiers, the two unidentified boys both died on a death train, Bernáth Weicker and Antal Reizner were sent to hard labor camps and then died in death camps. Péter Altman and the second Andor____ also both died in the Holocaust.

rectly. Each family member wrote his or her name on a piece of paper and made me keep saying it until I could pronounce it correctly. They were all happy that I could finally call them by name.

My mother was especially proud that I was learning, but I could tell she wasn't happy. I caught her crying and asked, "Why are you crying?" She said, "They've taken your brother, Miklós, to a hard-labor camp." She was also upset because the government had taken all of our wheat and corn and, as a result, it was becoming harder to survive let alone make a living. Although my mother didn't tell me at the time, the government had been quite busy confiscating farmland from the Jews in our area. In any case, we continued to endure the thirteen-kilometer trek to sell our dairy products for cash, grateful that we were all so very strong. Everyone was struggling, and bartering goods became commonplace, even for my family.

I spent the summer working and playing on the farm, as usual. Naturally, my chores and responsibilities had increased because I was getting older. One of my new chores was packing lunches with my sister. When we were done, we walked out to the fields where my family was hard at work to deliver them.

We children shared many of our chores, but some were separate. Every Thursday, my sisters would prepare enough dough to make bread and pastries to last one week. Friday mornings were set aside for the baking. My sisters molded the dough for the bread into seven round shapes and placed them all into our huge brick oven. The oven remained extremely hot after the breads and cakes were removed. Not wanting to waste the remaining oven heat, my sisters also prepared chulint every Friday afternoon. The chulint consisted of a mixture of meat and beans. After the chulint was placed in the oven, my sisters packed clay into the oven's opening to seal it. The chulint remained there for twenty-four hours.

One new chore that I truly enjoyed was fishing at the creek. Every Friday morning, my brothers sent me out to catch live flies for bait. Hiding low in the grassy fields, I waited for any opportunity to catch the bait with my bare hands. I carefully placed the captured flies, alive, into a matchbox. Then Salgo, Sándor, and I would go to the river and fish. Although we caught plenty of medium-sized fish, I always wished that we could land ones that were bigger.

After several trips to the creek, I asked Salgo how we could catch larger fish. He explained that the fly bait we were using was too small to catch the bigger fish and that we would need to use larger bait. The following Friday, I eagerly went out and attempted to capture live grasshoppers. Unfortunately, I was unable to catch them with my bare hands. They were much larger than flies and seemed a tad wiser. I knew I needed an alternative strategy.

The next time we went to the creek, I brought my hat. I waited patiently in the fields until I spotted a hoard of grasshoppers. I watched them intently, calculating their jumping distance. I couldn't grab them, so from a distance, I tossed my hat, which landed on a few, trapping them. My attempt was a success. My brothers used the grasshoppers, and my wish for bigger fish came true.

Whenever we got home from fishing, my mother immediately cleaned the catch. She promptly filleted the fish for the main course. With the leftover fish parts, she made bouillabaisse. Fish was served every Friday, no matter what. When the weather was bad and we were unable to bring home a catch, my mother sent us to the fish store near the mill to purchase our dinner.

However, before dinner, we got cleaned up and went to the local synagogue. Afterward, my father conducted additional prayers at the dinner table, a requirement before the dinner could be served. In my world of silence, my father's praying bored me, and often, I drifted off to sleep. I always received a tap on the shoulder to wake me up when dinner was served.

Reading the newspaper was the post-meal ritual. Being able to participate in the family discussions about news from the Hungarian national newspaper made me feel like an active member in my family. I constantly asked, "What's going on?" Our body language decreased and talking increased. As my communication improved, everybody began involving me in activities and conversations. At the institute, I had felt like a real person, but now with my family, I felt like a complete human being.

The feeling of wholeness gave me a renewed sense of energy. I wanted to do everything, and I did plenty. I rode a bicycle, rode the horse, played with the animals, and visited with my neighbors. I even went out of my way to speak with the postman. He was thrilled that I could speak. I don't believe his son had the ability. The villagers were impressed with how quickly I had learned.

We also went to the synagogue every Saturday morning. There were three Orthodox and two Conservative temples in the area. In the temple that we attended, boys and men were separated from girls and women. The females prayed on the top floor, and the men prayed on the bottom floor. Worship was extremely boring for me

A photograph of me circa 1943 that Magda kept on her wall.

because I couldn't hear let alone understand what was going on. I saw no purpose for my presence. In addition, I hated walking to and from the synagogue, particularly because it scared me. Arrow Cross militants walked around with their German shepherd dogs. The Arrow Cross members had trained the dogs to attack Jews because they enjoyed watching the dogs attack innocent people. I didn't enjoy their sick game. Because I couldn't hear, I had to rely on my acute vision to stay in tune with my surroundings. Even when it wasn't Saturday, my heart raced any time I was off the grounds of our farm.

After arriving home from the synagogue, my mother and sisters served the lunch. On Saturdays, we ate the chulint that had been placed in the brick oven the prior day. After lunch, we each took a nap. I looked forward to the darkness at the end of the day because it signified the end of the Sabbath, which in turn, allowed me more freedom.

As summer came to an end, I felt a great sense of fulfillment. My mother scraped together the earnings from our trips to the market to pay my way back to Budapest. Once again, she couldn't accompany me. Everybody said good-bye with the normal hugs and kisses. The train ride was smooth. During the trip, I reflected on my summer at home on the farm. I also eagerly looked forward to seeing my friends at the institute and to sharing with them all that I had done. Naturally, I was curious to know how they had spent their summer vacations.

Back at school, I was promoted to the third grade. My vocabulary was growing, and my writing skills were improving immensely. Sári néni continued to feed me new words and taught me how to create new sentences and how to compose letters. I also read. If I came across a word or phrase I didn't understand, I'd have to raise my hand, and she would explain it to me. Similarly, when we finished class, we went to the study hall where the older children talked, and if I saw a word I didn't know, I would stop the conversation and say, "Excuse me, what does this word mean?" Then, they told me and I learned from them.

All of these activities made it possible for me to read more of the newspaper and begin to understand more about adult politics. I remember wondering why the newspaper stated that nobody knew what to do with the Jews. It made me angry. The adults and counselors at the institute were constantly arguing over the politics of the war. We all knew that, at this point, the Hungarian and German Army had been victorious in invading Russia. I gave my opinions, too, based on what I knew.

CHAPTER 5 (1943–1944)

A SPECIAL TRIP HOME

IN THE DEAD of winter, just before Hanukkah, my parents sent a letter to the institute, requesting that I return home immediately. My parents heard from the community grapevine that the Polish Jews had been sent to Auschwitz and that they may be forced to go, too. Poland wasn't that far away. We were near the Polish border, anywhere from fifty to less than one hundred miles away. My parents must have had the feeling it might be the last time they would see me.

Dr. Kanizsai came to me with a somewhat frantic look on his face, telling me to pack my belongings as quickly as possible because I was going home. I believed that this homecoming was a special treat; however, Dr. Kanizsai and the counselors refused to explain why I had to leave so abruptly. I didn't know that this trip home would be the last one where I would see my entire family united.

Sári néni knew of my parent's request. In fact, it seemed as though Sári néni knew everything and beyond. She told me she felt anxious about my traveling alone because I would be arriving during the evening hours, and the institute had had no way during the hurried planning to notify my family of my arrival time. Sári néni anticipated that I would arrive at the train station with nobody to meet me and figured that I'd have to walk home from the station alone. She gave me a couple of packs of matches, which I placed in the left pocket of my jacket. If nobody was at the station to pick me up and I had to walk home alone, then I would need to light a match if wolves approached me, she warned. The newspaper had reported that the Carpathian region was experiencing an unusual deluge of wolves, she explained. But, she added, the wolves were afraid of fire. Sári néni made me feel prepared.

I arrived at the train station but couldn't get on the train because it was so full of people. The people were pushing and shoving to get on board. While waiting to see what would happen next, I noticed to my surprise that all the people started getting off the train. I guessed that the trip had been cancelled, so I went back to the institute. One of the counselors approached me and said, "What happened?" I responded, "I couldn't get on the train." "This is a big problem," said the counselor, but he added, "Don't worry. Tomorrow we'll get you a seat." So, the next day, the counselor accompanied me to the train station and physically put me on a seat on the train. The trip was not cancelled this time, and I was finally on my way home.

This train ride home was different. I had traveled by train only during the day and only in the fall and summer months. Now, the scenery, smell, and feelings were foreign to me. When I arrived at the station, I was excited that my father and Jolán were there waiting. I showed them the matches Sári néni had given me. My father laughed and Jolán nodded with approval, saying, "Good."

The three of us walked home that night in pitch-black darkness. Fortunately, my father had brought along my snowshoes because the snow was piled high. They were constructed out of cut-up logs and nails. The air temperature was cold—minus twenty degrees Celsius—and I felt the chill down to my bones.

When we got to the house, my mother embraced me extra firmly. Tears were streaming down her face. Her emotions appeared more intense at this homecoming than for any other visit that I had made home. I was still unaware of the serious and immediate danger to my family's wellness and survival.

During my stay, I noticed that every being on the farm appeared worn out, from my family to our farm animals. Our pregnant horse had become ill from being overworked, continuously and solely hauling fertilizer back and forth from the compost heap to the fields. My mother called the veterinarian. I began to worry that our horse would die, along with her unborn colt. The horse had beads of sweat all over her body. The veterinarian insisted that we force-feed her honey and bread. I stroked her while my mother made her as comfortable as possible. That same night, around eleven o'clock, the horse rose to her feet. She had come back to life.

Toward the end of my approximate three-week visit, Jolán took me on a ten-mile horse-and-sleigh journey through the snow. We went to visit my schoolmate, Leó Wachtenheim, and to meet with his family. Both of our families wanted us to travel together for our journey back to the institute. The journey to Leó's home was a fantastic adventure. The horse and sleigh skimmed with ease through the powdery snow. Rarely was I able to venture off the farm during my visits, except to go to the synagogue on Friday nights and Saturday mornings. Jolán and I stayed for only a short time, just long enough for Leó's parents and Jolán to finalize the upcoming travel arrangements for Leó and me.

Back at home, my mother promised me that I could visit the family again during the springtime break for Passover. I was pleased that I would be able to come home again before summertime, especially, because I would then be able see the colt that would be born in February. Several days later, I met Leó at the train station, and we were off to Budapest. I particularly enjoyed having a companion with whom I could easily communicate for the train ride. We arrived at the institute safe and sound. Once back, I appreciated the institute's modern conveniences such as indoor toilets. At home, I had had to use a chamber pot because it was too cold to go outside to the outhouse.

The remainder of my winter holiday was spent idly at the institute. Saturdays were busier than other days. On Saturday mornings, all the children from third through seventh grade were required to go to the synagogue. Those children in grades kindergarten through second were not required to attend. The synagogue was located across the street in a public girls school. Saturday evenings were designated as movie night. We had to earn our way to the movies, which meant that we were required to be on our very best behavior at all times. If any of us displayed poor behavior during school, or even at the movies, we were restricted from going to the movies the following week. On one particular day, I had behaved poorly and was restricted from going to the next movie outing. Angry, I threatened one of my counselors, proclaiming that I would tell my mother that

I received unfair punishment. However, I made sure that I never missed another movie outing. When movie time came, all the children who had been good were called to line up in two single files and march in this formation for the two-block trek to the movie theater and its special fun.

Winter vacation finally ended, and school resumed again. Some of the children complained about Dr. Kanizsai, but we knew we shouldn't talk about him. One young man named Sándor Weicker and another student, Andor Striker, fled from the institute to the police department, complaining about abuse from Dr. Kanizsai. The police sent them back to the institute without any assistance. For four days in a row after that incident, Weicker and Striker received slaps in the face from Dr. Kanizsai during our routine morning fingernail cleanliness check. Dr. Kanizsai regularly spanked the children when they defied him. I never got spanked by him, and as a precaution, I tried to talk to him diplomatically.

Dr. Kanizsai was not the only person to hit students. A fifth-grade teacher named Ignácz Kardos regularly lost patience and smacked the students who had trouble learning. They feared him. Kardos spanked Jancsi so much that he was afraid to learn. One day, Kardos brought a girl and boy student into my classroom. He asked Péter and I to respond to a question. When we both came up with the correct response, Kardos turned to his two students and said, "Look. They can answer the question correctly and you cannot. Maybe I should put you both back in third grade and promote Péter and Izráel to fifth grade." Unfortunately, many students suffered under Kardos's teaching.

As school continued, I anxiously waited for the promised letter from my mother that would let me know when I could return home for Passover. I drove Sári néni crazy every time I saw the postman. Sári néni tried to console me, telling me that the mail service was often delayed because border access was limited during the ongoing war. Even though her explanation was true, Sári néni knew the real reason why I did not receive any word. She was aware of my family's plight and kept their situation a secret.

Up until this point in 1944, Admiral Horthy believed that the Hungarian Jews were Hungary's responsibility. Throughout Europe, Jews were total outcasts, except in Hungary. But now, with pressure from the rest of Europe, the hatred toward Jews had crept into the city of Budapest. Now, businesses owned by Jews were being shut down, and all Jews were prohibited from making a living.[1] Dr. Kanizsai was aware of the imminent danger and did what he could do to protect us from being deported.

By March 19, 1944, German divisions had moved into Hungary.[2] Even after following all the newspaper headlines, I still had no suspicion, not even the slightest clue, that mass genocide was occurring in other parts of Europe, and I never read anything about how deaf people were being treated. I certainly did not expect what was coming next for Hungary.

Soon, however, I began realizing what was happening. I worried about my family and about their safety. I worried about myself and about what I should do. I pondered how the world could permit this exploitation. I wondered whether the world was deaf and blind. I questioned the religiosity of all people, especially churchgoers, who claimed to believe in God. I knew they had to be hypocrites because they were not following the Ten Commandments. Their actions were entirely heartless and inhumane toward Jews. I was angry that nobody was helping.

In my despair and anger, I was unaware that, during this rampant deportation, a Swedish diplomat named Raoul Wallenberg had already successfully saved almost 20,000 Hungarian Jews by providing each one with Swedish identification. Anyone who held this identification was allowed to leave Hungary under the diplomatic protection of Sweden, which was a neutral party in the war. Unfortunately, I am not aware of anyone from our institute who was offered this help.

CHAPTER **6** (1944)

THE YELLOW STAR OF DAVID
AND THE RED CROSS

SEVERAL WEEKS passed after the order that shut down all Jewish businesses, and on April 5, 1944, the Hungarian government made another order for all Jews.[1] We were now required to identify ourselves as Jews by wearing a yellow Star of David placed on the left side of our chests. The government didn't provide the stars, so the girls from the institute cut and sewed yellow cloth stars for all of us children. Children and adults alike were required to wear the yellow Star of David at all times. I felt odd having to identify myself as a Jew. The new practice was the beginning effort to make Hungary Judenfrei—a territory free of Jews. Dr. Kanizsai warned us that if any of us disobeyed or forgot the order to wear the yellow star and were found out to be a Jew, we would be shot without question. I wondered whether my family back home also had to wear the yellow stars.

After we received the order requiring us to identify ourselves, another new order was issued. All Jews now had to obey special curfews that were imposed at inconsistent times of the day. We were most often allowed to walk outdoors only between the hours of two and four o'clock in the afternoon. If we were caught before or after a curfew time, we'd be shot down, without question. Even at the non-curfew times, we weren't safe to wander outside the institute. Adults and children who were anti-Semitic would throw rocks, bottles, and whatever else they could get their hands on to torment and injure us Jews.

Passover came and went, without a letter from my family, without a word. I felt so frustrated and helpless. Nobody would tell me what was going on. Even though I understood the newspapers more and could get involved in some political discussions, I still had many questions.

41

The Gentiles became more and more contemptuous toward us Jews. They felt as though we Jews were responsible for all of their inequities, including differences in education. For example, Budapest had two competing deaf schools—the government school and our Jewish institute. To my surprise, we were pushed into an academic competition in the midst of the surrounding turmoil. The children from the government school, who were in the seventh grade, were forced to compete academically against the fifth graders from our Jewish institute—a bizarre arrangement. Our institute won all the challenges against the government school.

We were happy, but we had no idea of the repercussion we would receive for being victorious. Oddly, shortly after the competition, our institute was shut down. Many people suspected that Kálmán Füzes was the instigator in our institute's closure. He had a stake in the competition and was extremely bitter about losing all the challenges. He was a teacher who was also an Arrow Cross member and a sympathizer of the Fascist regime.

After our institute was closed, it was converted into the city police department. All of us children were temporarily separated. Those who had parents alive and were still in contact with them were sent home. The rest of us were sent to a Jewish orphanage that was located on Vilma Királynö (Queen Wilma Street) in Budapest.

I had no choice or say about what would happen to me. I had no way of knowing whether my parents or family members were still alive because I hadn't received any correspondence. Even if my family were alive, the borders along the Carpathian region had been closed off. Consequently, whether or not they had survived, I was stuck. But Péter wasn't. Péter's mother felt that he would be safer at home with her, so he was sent home. To me, Péter was the lucky one, and I envied him deeply.

Although I didn't know it at the time, once Péter arrived in his hometown of Orosháza, he was reunited only briefly with his mother. The two of them were herded into a ghetto with 900 other Jews. By June, they were set aboard the death train heading for Auschwitz. Fortunately for them, the train tracks that led to Auschwitz had been bombed, which forced the death train to be rerouted to Austria, buying them some valuable time. They would remain in a detention center until December.

My situation was entirely different. My new home was the orphanage, which housed primarily hearing children. About thirty of us boys and girls were deaf. The building was huge. Half the building was designated for the hearing girls, and the other half was allocated for the hearing boys. The hearing children were grouped fifteen to a room. All of us deaf boys were grouped together in one room in the boys' half of the building, and all the deaf girls were placed into one room in the girls' half of the building.

Kardos, the fifth-grade teacher at our institute, was aware that we were in the orphanage. He also knew the orphanage could provide us with meals only Monday through Friday. He went door to door in search of Jews in the 7th District who would provide us with a wholesome dinner on Saturdays and Sundays, and he was successful.

Although we were in tight quarters, I thought the orphanage was very good. They served excellent food and had their own infirmary. I felt that I was going to be okay and prayed that life would get back to normal. I also prayed for news from my family.

By early May 1944, most of the Hungarian Jews had been deported or killed, no thanks to Rudolph Kastner, a Jew who arranged with Eichmann to save several thousand Jews in exchange for a list of names of Jews to be sent to death camps.[2] He was a traitor. Approximately 450,000 Hungarian Jews had been rounded up by the Arrow Cross Party and police and had been deported to Nazi death camps. Many humanitarian groups had protested, but they were all powerless.

Also in May, as I was playing out in the yard of the orphanage, I noticed British and American planes flying overhead. As I looked around, I saw the counselors waving their hands, frantically motioning all of us to follow them. We followed them down to the bomb shelter where we remained for a brief fifteen minutes. When we exited the shelter, the counselors told us that the alarm had been a false air raid. They explained that the planes were taking aerial photos of Budapest and the surrounding area. Although we were told it was not serious, we were warned that if any planes were to pass again, we had to return to the bomb shelter.

A few days went by, and once again, planes flew overhead. But this time, instead of a handful of planes, what appeared to be hundreds of planes crowded the sky. We all evacuated the building, heading directly to the bomb shelter. This time, the air raid was for real. In an instant, the planes began bombing. I watched as the counselors instructed the hearing children to place their hands over their ears and hold them there while keeping their mouths open. We deaf children followed exactly what the hearing children were doing.

The building began shaking like we were having an earthquake. Then, the big bomb came with a direct hit to our building. Each floor came collapsing down, floor by floor, to the ground level. The lights flickered. Pushing and shoving, we panicked, trying to exit the building. I made it to the staircase, crawling up toward the door. The cloud of dust made it impossible to see. I felt my way up to the building's main floor and continued to crawl upward until I made it out to the yard.

I was so relieved that I had made my way out of the building. As soon as the dust settled, I saw that the boys' section of the building had been flattened completely. The girls' section had been spared, although it was uninhabitable. All of us children from the orphanage, deaf and hearing alike, were now homeless. We survivors quickly regrouped and decided that we needed to save ourselves immediately. We began marching in the streets shouting, "Who will adopt me?" I hadn't marched for five minutes when one family spotted me and immediately took me in. The couple had only one child—a hearing son. I wondered why they had no other children. We got along very well, and they were very kind and generous to me. Sometimes, I felt as though they had rescued me so their son would have a playmate. But whatever the reason, they took me in. I was temporarily safe and extremely grateful.

During the period of May through early July, the 450,000 Hungarian Jews who had been herded onto the 148 deportation trains had arrived at the gas chambers at Auschwitz-Birkenau. During the train ride, many people died and suffered from injuries. The people had been packed in the train cars like sardines in cans. Once they arrived at Auschwitz, many were ushered immediately into the gas chamber where they were killed. Those who didn't get sent to the chambers right away received other types of treatments. In the name of science, medical experiments were being performed without anesthesia. The experiments were cruel and inhumane. Rape and torture were common practices. Among the Fascists, only a deep jealousy, hatred, and ignorance prevailed toward Jews, disabled people, and those who were humane enough to speak up for civil rights.

Admiral Horthy began worrying about the deportations and what the world might think.[3] He wasn't happy with the situation and decided to stand up to Eichmann. Eichmann was Hungary's nightmare and, like Hitler, was despicable. Horthy wanted to take back control of his country and save his own neck. His solution was to sign an order ending deportations, and Eichmann was enraged.

My stay with the family who adopted me ended after only two weeks. Sári néni had gone out to search for me. She quickly learned what had happened to the orphanage. Making a risky move, she showed up at my adopted family's home and claimed me as part of her family. Sári néni instructed me to place my yellow Star of David badge in my shirt pocket and warned me against using sign language, advising that if I had something to say, I must use oral methods. She told me that we were going to her home on the "Buda" side of Budapest where people were primarily of German descent. She warned me that the star was a danger to both of us because Buda was infested with Arrow Cross militants and Nazis. She sternly told me not to tell anyone that I was Jewish. Any Jews who remained in Buda were in hiding. Thus, I would be in hiding, too.

Sári néni was more than my teacher. She was my true friend. She and her extended family warmly accepted me and were kind and generous. Now I would have not only a chance at survival but also comfortable living arrangements. My new home allowed me to know Sári néni on a more personal level. I already knew that she was Jewish, young, and attractive. Soon I learned that she was also a chain-smoker and an espresso drinker. In fact, she was never without either. She always wore a full mink coat, regardless of the weather. And sadly, she was a widow who had been married for only two months to a doctor who then died of cancer.

Sári néni's home stood four stories high and was lavishly decorated. The Balkányi family (Sári néni's mother) and the Marcus family (Sári néni's mother's sister) shared the home. Sári néni and I slept on the first floor. The second and third floors were also sleeping areas, which were occupied by the remaining family members. The fourth floor housed the entertainment area, kitchen, dining room, and living room.

Sári néni's mother was wonderful. In fact, the whole family was wonderful. They had maids and a black woman chef. They were rich. Sári néni's father, Kálmán Balkányi, was very much involved in law and business. He was a famous attorney and was involved in Parliament where he served as treasurer. His signature was on the inflation pengő currency of 1946 and 1947. Sári néni's uncle was involved in the Hungarian-British banking industry.

I felt extremely lucky to be staying with Sári néni and her family. They taught me how to be respectful, how to kiss a hand, how to eat with a knife and fork, and how to be a gentleman. Because I liked it so much, I learned quickly. But I could not forget my own family. I regularly pestered Sári néni for news about them. She finally broke down one day, telling me that my entire family most likely had been rounded up by the Arrow Cross Party and sent to either a hard-labor camp or a concentration camp. I prayed regularly for my family's safety and survival, but though I didn't know it at the time, by July 1944, most of the Hungarian Jews were dead.[4] I remained with the Balkányis for a few months, until approximately August.

In August, Romania lost its control to the Russian army. The Arrow Cross militants began searching wall to wall throughout Buda for any remaining Jews in hiding. The Balkányi family was anxious about my presence. They felt that I could no longer remain at their home. The Balkányi families had immunity from the Hungarian government. However, if the Fascists found them harboring any Jew or fugitive, their immunity would be jeopardized and they, too, would fall victim to the hate crimes of the war. They had to let me go to fend for myself. Although the family tried to comfort me, I was extremely frightened. They gave me fifty pengő to help me out. Sári néni gave me the yellow star to put back on my chest. Then, the Balkányis and I parted sadly.

Sári néni took me back to Pest and dropped me off at the Red Cross camp, which had been the city's police department and, prior to that, our school. I have no idea how long the Red Cross personnel had been there. However, I was surprised and somewhat comforted to know that the Red Cross camp had been set up at our school. I knew the building and its surroundings. At least I had my bearings. I worried about Sári néni and her family. They weren't safe either. She and her family would eventually have to go into hiding in some farm town. They could afford to pay for protection.

I didn't know it at the time, but Raoul Wallenberg, under the auspices of the Swedish government, had set up the Red Cross camp. In a short time, he had accomplished incredible acts. The Swedish government had supplied Wallenberg with a limited number of Swedish neutral passports to give to the Jews to make them appear Swedish. However, he soon needed more and needed them quickly. Knowing that he would not be able to get what he needed through diplomatic channels soon enough, he decided to make fake passes, which he called Schutzpasses. The Arrow Cross Party and the Nazis did not question the validity of Wallenberg's fake passes. All the passes combined saved nearly 100,000 Jews during the war. Wallenberg's regret was that he had not started earlier.[5] In Budapest, people who knew of the Schutzpass searched feverishly for any link they could find between themselves and someone in Sweden. Having a connection with someone in Sweden made getting the pass easier.

When I entered the Red Cross building, the smell of disinfectant was intoxicating. The building didn't have the homey smell I had been accustomed to. Disinfectant was being used everywhere to combat the rampant diseases that afflicted the people throughout the city. Overall, the sanitary conditions were poor. Reaching the yard at the rear of the building, I was stunned. The empty field looked like a military camp. Makeshift wood structures and tents were scattered throughout. The Red Cross basically had established a concentration camp, which housed Red Cross personnel, approximately 100 deaf Jewish children and adults—including anywhere from thirty to forty students from the institute—and approximately 750 Jews from the general populous. I didn't know most of the people. None of the school children questioned why there were other people at our school. I don't know why I didn't ask. Hearing people mingled with deaf people, and we were all mixed up. I spotted Dr. Kanizsai, who was surrounded by children. The Red Cross had appointed him to be in charge of the children. I let him know I had returned, happy to be able to use sign language again. I admired his diligence in continuing to stick by all of us.

The Red Cross camp was set up as a safe haven. They provided us with shelter and food. Members of the Arrow Cross Party were not permitted to enter. I remembered when I had seen the Arrow Cross militants at home on the Sabbath; they used the command "Jewish" to get their well-trained dogs to attack. Arrow Cross members looked like Nazis, and their eyes were constantly alert for Jews—like wolves' eyes searching for prey. I knew I had to be on guard around those in the Arrow Cross Party, so I was relieved that they could not enter. However, outside the camp's perimeters, they waited. The curfew was still in force, and anyone who disobeyed the order would be shot on sight. Unfortunately, György Eiland, a seventh-grade student from our institute, was shot to death for breaking curfew.

All markets, bakeries, and stores were not permitted to sell their goods to us Jews. But the Jewish people kept insisting, and the stores wanted to make money. So, store owners willing to risk disobeying the government sold their goods at a dear cost. Store owners who got caught making these sales would either lose their businesses or be arrested. Any Jew caught making a purchase would be shot on sight. My food came from the Red Cross. Although it was safe, it was bland, and I constantly dreamt about having flavorful meals.

A week or so after arriving at the camp, I began observing a man selling cakes. He was buying the cakes from the bakery across the street. I knew the cakes were only sixty fillérs apiece (one hundred fillérs equals one pengő). But, he was selling them to the people at the Red Cross for one hundred and twenty fillérs! I was very impressed and contemplated long and hard about selling the cakes, too. I knew my disadvantage was my being a Jew, but I had been told I looked like a Christian. The man selling the cakes was a Gentile. I wondered about how I could hide my identity. The simple solution was to remove the yellow star from my chest. I realized that I was risking my life to lie about my identity and sell the cakes to other Jews. But, I rationalized, a Gentile selling to a Jew could not be any worse than a Jew selling to a Jew. I also realized that I would have to risk breaking curfew because the cakes were made early in the morning. I made whatever rationalizations I needed to make, and I decided to take the risk.

The owners of the bakery knew that I was Jewish because they had known me before as a student from the institute. They liked me and decided to keep quiet, acting ignorant about my identity and taking the risk of selling me the cakes. With the money I had from the Balkányi family, I decided to start off by buying fifty cakes for sixty fillérs apiece and selling them at one hundred and twenty fillérs apiece, just as the other man had done. The man sold only one type of cake, so I decided to sell two kinds—a walnut torte and a poppy-seed strudel.

My first day of cake sales was very successful. I was amazed at how quickly the cakes sold, all within ten minutes. The people in the streets and from the Red Cross bought more from me than from the other man. Perhaps they took pity on me because of my deaf-orphan status. So, I quickly went back to the bakery and bought some more. I was successful once again, selling every single cake.

After that first day, I regularly made two or three trips each day, carrying fifty pieces of cake at a time. I ripped up cardboard to use as a tray to carry the cakes. Every day, the baker encouraged me to come back the next day to buy more cakes. My customers got disappointed when I ran out of cakes. Some days, I had a few left over, so I ate them myself.

The bakery owners began to rely on my business. I had regular customers. Mrs. Weltner, a Jewish hearing woman, always bought the most cakes, making a fuss over me as she bought them. I didn't know it at the time, but she had a deaf son, György, who was also in the ghetto. György ended up as a survivor, but his mother died in a camp in Germany.

After several weeks of selling cakes, I decided to sell newspapers, too. I sold cakes in the morning and newspapers in the evening. The newspaper, the *Evening Bulletin*, cost me twenty fillérs each, and I sold each one for forty fillérs. Selling the paper was a blessing because I could read some of the political events. Night after night, the headlines would read, "What to Do with the Jews?" The paper also had stories about a black market and people buying bread at double and triple prices. Within the ghetto, the price of bread was ten times the regular amount. I knew I had to save my money in case I ended up in the ghetto.

More and more people poured into the confines of the camp. I continued selling cakes and newspapers for a couple of months, making thousands of pengős. I began feeling stronger, independent, and less in need of Dr. Kanizsai. But I missed not seeing Sári néni, and I kept up my prayers for my family.

Those couple months were idyllic compared to what lay ahead. Life changed suddenly one night while I was asleep in the Red Cross building. American planes were busy flying overhead. I was dreaming of being at home in the summer when the ground would tremble from the thunder. I awoke in a deep sweat. Looking around the room, I felt disoriented and realized that all the beds were empty. I rushed to the window and saw aerial fighting lighting up the night sky. The Fascists on the ground were shooting at the planes flying above. The scene looked like a fireworks display. I watched in awe as the planes fell out of the air, exploding as they hurdled down. I realized that the thunder in my dream had been the actual shaking from the bombs and planes hitting the ground. I quickly ran down to the bomb shelter, disappointed that nobody had bothered to wake me up. As soon as I made it to the shelter, a Red Cross worker began to interrogate me. Dr. Kanizsai stepped forward and explained that I was one of his students. We all stayed in the shelter until the bombing ceased.

The next morning, we exited the shelter. The sky was full of smoke, and the air held a horrendous burning odor. Dr. Kanizsai announced to us that the Red Cross personnel were recommending that everyone receive immunizations. I received three shots, one each in my stomach, chest, and back. For what, I don't know. I felt like a pin cushion.

CHAPTER 7 (1944)

TEARS OF JOY AND DESPAIR

IN THE MEANTIME, Admiral Horthy became adamant about pulling Hungary out of the war. He sent a special envoy to Moscow to negotiate the terms of Hungary's surrender to the Russians. However, the Russian army had already arrived just south of Budapest, so Horthy's envoy had no bargaining power. He made an agreement with Russian officials that he would announce Hungary's withdrawal from the war on October 18, but he decided to move the date forward to October 15 when he learned that a Hungarian army general had been kidnapped.

On October 15, 1944, dramatic changes started taking place. Admiral Horthy was planning his armistice announcement, unaware that his son had already been abducted by Nazi kidnappers earlier that day.[1] At the Red Cross camp, I began noticing people urgently shushing one another and huddling around a radio. Dr. Kanizsai made an announcement, saying that Horthy was calling for an armistice. Tears of joy began to flow from the eyes of both Hungarian Gentiles and Jews. Jews came pouring out of their marked homes, ripping off their yellow stars. I ripped mine off, too. We started a fire and threw in our stars, adding to the enormous blaze.

Then, another announcement came that the Hungarian soldiers were to distribute arms to the Jewish people who had been forced into hard labor. While we were celebrating, nobody knew that several German divisions had moved into the capital and that the royal palace had been surrounded. Horthy's 200 personal bodyguards from his elite troop worked hard to stave off the Nazis, but the elite troop failed at fending off the German tanks. The battle lasted only a couple of hours. The Nazis prevailed. Unfortunately, Horthy's armistice never had a chance.

Once again, the people huddled around the radio. I couldn't find Dr. Kanizsai. The news bulletin began, and the hearing people tried to orally explain the situation to me. A woman explained that music from the Fascists' regime was being played and that, once again, Budapest was at the mercy of the Nazis and the Arrow Cross Party. Our fear escalated when we realized that many of us had thrown away or burned our yellow stars. The tears that flowed now were from sorrow and despair.

Even though the Germans had successfully overtaken the royal palace, they threatened Horthy to formally withdraw his armistice announcement or else they would kill his son. They also forced Horthy to announce that Ferenc Szálasi was now the new leader of the Arrow Cross Party and Hungary's new head of government.[2] The Nazis decided to keep Horthy under house arrest in the palace, with his son remaining in a hard-labor camp.

Ferenc Szálasi wielded his new power quickly. His strategy to deport Jews and other undesirables started in earnest. The people of Budapest were terrified. Dozens of Jews were being taken to the Duna Folyó (Danube River) where they were shot and dumped into the freezing water.[3] Everything was in disarray. Dr. Kanizsai encouraged all of us to remain under the protection of the Red Cross.

After a few days had passed, someone tipped off the Arrow Cross Party that forty-five Jewish partisans were hiding in the Red Cross camp. At about five o'clock in the morning, Arrow Cross militants entered the building. Most of us were sleeping. Knowing that partisans were possibly being hidden, the Arrow Cross troops ignored the sign posted by the Red Cross, which indicated immunity. They ripped the sign off the building and began banging a bell, shouting, "Everyone out!"[4] Not knowing what was going on, I followed along with what everyone else was doing. I quickly packed up my belongings, stashed my money in my underwear, and followed everyone out of the building.

Once we were all outside, Arrow Cross militants ordered us to line up. Everybody was paralyzed with fear that the Arrow Cross

Party had shown up. The commotion was overwhelming. We were all stunned. We lost our heads. I could neither sign nor talk. Even the hearing people couldn't talk. We were all speechless. In a way, our silence was good because if we had spoken, they most likely would have shot us.

We were told to place all of our possessions, money, and jewelry in specially designated redwood collection boxes that were being shoved in our faces. The Arrow Cross troops checked everyone's mouth for gold fillings, which they pulled out without hesitation. However, they weren't checking everyone's pockets. I had thousands of pengős hidden in my underwear from months of selling cakes and newspapers. I decided to take a risk and not put the money into the collection box. Luckily, I was never searched. Then, the Arrow Cross soldiers told us to prepare to move to another location. Some people hugged, some cried, and others prayed. Some people seemed lifeless, overcome that their lives might end soon.

Several hours later, my fate was revealed. The Arrow Cross troops decided to modify their orders. Anyone who was disabled, elderly, bedridden, and so forth was to stay put. My friends and I were safe— ironically, blessed for being deaf.

We were then commanded to reenter the building and proceed up to the second floor. My friends and I were sitting around when, all of a sudden, shots erupted, which sounded to me like faint buzzing sounds. The partisans on the roof and the Arrow Cross troops on the street were shooting at one another. I had no idea how the partisans had gotten into the building, whether or not they had been hiding out, or any other details about their presence. I just knew they were there and that they had created a problem for the rest of us. The Arrow Cross troops entered the building and ordered everyone to put up their hands. They wanted to find the partisans. As I turned around to read the lips of an Arrow Cross officer, he kicked me in the rear with his hard, steel-toed boots. The kick left me bruised and swollen. He ordered everyone, including myself, to go down the steps and out into the street to stand in front of a trolley car with our hands up.

We had to get in line again. An Arrow Cross officer scanned the line, looking for the nine partisans who had been shooting from the rooftop. The Arrow Cross militants identified the partisans and began beating them harshly. I knew they were the partisans only because the Arrow Cross officers were saying, "These are the partisans." Otherwise, I wouldn't have known a partisan from an average person. We were all forced to watch as each partisan was kicked and stepped on. Their bodies were bleeding from every orifice. I was sickened by the brutality. I later learned that these Jewish partisans were known as rebels or resisters. They were the few Jews who would fight back.

Then, the Arrow Cross ordered that we all divide ourselves into two groups. The first group was for those who appeared to be fifteen years and older. With my hands still up in the air, I began to cry. A woman in line sternly said to me, "Don't cry." Although I couldn't help but think about the fate of my parents, I had to stop crying. I had to hold my feelings inside of me. My fears were for my parents' safety, not for myself. Then, an Arrow Cross officer pulled Sándor Weicker out of the line. He wasn't older than fifteen, but they obviously had assumed he was in that category. He was only in fifth grade! Those who were selected were deported to Germany, Austria, or Poland by cattle train. I survived by ending up in the younger group. My group was sent back inside the building. Once again, I felt spared, yet I was no longer under the protection of the Red Cross.

The next day, I looked around for Leó. A friend of mine told me that Leó had been shot to death. He told me it had happened when we had been ordered to go outside. Leó had been heading down the staircase when an Arrow Cross officer ordered him to halt. Because he was deaf, Leó didn't hear the officer's command. The officer shot Leó six times in his back. As each shot was fired, Leó's body flip-flopped down the staircase. I was lucky only to have gotten kicked in the rear. My heart pounded when I realized that each moment, each breath could produce a near-death experience. I realized yesterday's shooting could have been me, not Leó.

The following day, I awoke to an Arrow Cross officer shaking me and yelling in my face to get up. Once again, we were all ordered to form a line. We were instructed to clean the building thoroughly and be packed up by noon. The Arrow Cross troops were planning to move us to another location. Their announcement was accompanied by a threatening message: If we were not finished cleaning the building by the noon departure time, we would all be gunned down. The order to clean everything by noon seemed like an impossible task, but we all pitched in and helped one another. The task wasn't easy because I was weak from lack of food and exposure to the cold.

The Arrow Cross militants had planned to take all of us to Germany and kill us. Fortunately, when noon arrived, nothing happened. The Arrow Cross soldiers shuffled around, scratching their heads, unsure about their plans. We didn't know that the Russians had surrounded the area and were only ten kilometers away. The Arrow Cross's plan to get rid of us had failed.

A few days passed, and once more, the Arrow Cross troops told us we were moving. Of course, none of us knew where we were headed. We were forced to walk six kilometers in the cold—not an easy undertaking with my one pair of rubber shoes. I had no socks or stockings, and I had to wrap my feet in towels and sheets. My feet were frostbitten, but I knew if I limped or took a short rest, I'd be shot. I continued on in the bitter cold.

CHAPTER **8** (1944–1945)

THE CENTRAL GHETTO AND
THE CHRISTMAS NIGHTMARE

WE ARRIVED at Klauzal Square, within an area known as Zone Seven, or the Central Ghetto—now a ghost town. None of us knew that thousands of Jews had been interned in this area. It was a fenced-in area, completely filled with abandoned apartment buildings. Some of the apartments were damaged from the bombing whereas others were still intact. We saw no people. Dr. Kanizsai instructed us to try and stay together as a group. No living arrangements had been made for any of us.

Dr. Kanizsai went in search of an apartment for us children to sleep in for the night. It was an impossible task. All the apartments had been stripped completely—no furniture, heaters, blankets— absolutely nothing. I had to sleep on the concrete floor. The bathrooms were located outside the building. The stench of the ghetto was atrocious. Worst of all, we had no food or water. I was hungry, tired, and cold. That night, I almost froze to death.

By the next day, I was starving. Everyone spent the day searching for food. That night seemed colder than ever. Through the night, my body shivered and my stomach growled. Dr. Kanizsai continued searching for food.

The following day, I noticed some laborers had come to our area and had set up a table. The Arrow Cross Party had decided to provide us with a bit of something. Everyone rushed to the table, pushing one another to get there first. Dr. Kanizsai called order to the group, instructing everyone to form a line. I received my first cup of extremely bitter black coffee. The coffee was made from barley, not coffee beans. But that didn't matter because the heat from the coffee warmed my hands and my insides. The coffee made me hungrier.

I wished that I had never complained about the bland food from the Red Cross.

After we had our bitter coffee, Dr. Kanizsai informed us that we could no longer stay in the apartment building. More people were expected to enter the ghetto. We sought out shelter again in another abandoned apartment building. We still had no blankets, sheets, or heaters. I searched the building for whatever I could find. Jancsi, the fifth-grade student, and I stumbled on a blanket at the same moment. Jancsi was bigger than I was. I fought him for the blanket. Even though I was in third grade, I was very strong from all my farm work. I held out and won, ending up with one blanket and many cuts and bruises. I would have shared the blanket, but it was small.

That night, I laid my prize on the cold concrete floor, lying on one half and folding the other half over my body. Settled inside the blanket, I reflected on my fight with Jancsi. I now realized the meaning of survival. We were all on our own, and I might have to fight with other Jewish people to make it through, like I had done for the blanket.

Several more days passed, and I was desperate for food and heat. My nerves were on end, my stomach was growling, and my skin burned from the bitter cold. Finally, Dr. Kanizsai found us a permanent place on the cross streets of Wessélenyi Street and Akácfa Street. He was able to get a bit of food, which was really nothing. We did have some water in our apartment though. We took up residency throughout the building in different rooms and on different floors. I was assigned sleeping quarters on the second floor. Dr. Kanizsai and another counselor ordered me to start cleaning the second floor, room by room. The floor was covered with human feces, and we had no hot water with which to clean it up. I had to use cold water, which cleaned the floor but didn't get rid of the smell. When I was done, the counselor brought me lunch. He told Dr. Kanizsai to give me a pat on the back because I had worked very hard. He also suggested that I be given an extra ration of food for my efforts.

A couple days later, the bomb siren went off. Dr. Kanizsai rounded us up, instructing us to head down to the basement. In the basement, I could feel the violent shaking. It was scary. We were now in the dark because the building had lost its electricity. Once it was safe to come out of the basement, we could see the destruction. The bomb had destroyed the fourth, third, and second floors of the building. We had been saved by going to the basement in more ways than one. While down there, we discovered beds and blankets. Dr. Kanizsai assigned us to separate quarters in the basement. I was relieved and could now rest.

We still had no heat and little food. I began using my previously earned money to buy bread from Christians. One loaf of bread cost one hundred and twenty pengős. I hid some of my money under my mattress, which got stolen. The money for bread lasted for approximately one month.

During these months of November and December 1944, Budapest was in a state of lawlessness. Gangs of Arrow Cross officers roamed the streets, shooting anyone or anything in sight. Everyone was cold and starving, including many of the military men. Food, water, and heat were luxury items. A kilo of bread was worth eighty pengő on the black market. Christian inhabitants sold their goods to the people of the ghetto. My daily breakfast consisted of bitter black coffee. We had no real breakfast, lunch, or dinner. I had to search for food, eating primarily sugar beets and potatoes and, sometimes, animal feed. I even ate old food from the garbage cans and leftovers from the Arrow Cross officers. I constantly reminisced about my earlier days when I had been a picky eater. I vowed to myself that, if I survived, I would eat anything that was offered to me.

Enduring from day to day, just trying to stay alive, I had plenty of time to reflect on the events and people in my life. I wondered what had happened to my school friend, Péter. Although I was unaware of his plight when he had gone home in May, I later learned that around this time period, he had been deported to a concentration camp in the Netherlands named Bergen-Belsen. Both he and his mother had been separated. In the camp, Péter met a teenage boy named Pavel. Pavel could see that Péter was signing frantically as he was searching to find his mother. Pavel was a hearing son of deaf Poles. Pavel saved

Péter's life by telling him not to sign. Pavel knew that if any Fascist guard saw Péter using sign language, Péter would surely be killed.

Weeks passed and I just wanted to die. All my prayers to God seemed to be in vain. The winter was freezing and deadly, and the health of the people worsened. I was fortunate to have received the immunizations from the Red Cross to protect me from the infectious environment. People were weak, sick, and lice-infested. Many had already died. The dead bodies had a putrid smell. As soon as the dead bodies were removed, new ones appeared. Sometimes the bodies would remain a couple of days. Whenever Dr. Kanizsai saw a dead body, he ordered the older children to lift it and take it away. I have no idea where they went, how they disposed of them, or whether or not the bodies were buried or cremated. I began to grow accustomed to the smell. Newcomers were sick to their stomachs when they first entered the ghetto. The only time the smell was wretched to me was when I reentered the ghetto after the Arrow Cross militants had me work in the snow outside the ghetto walls. Then the smell was heightened.

My guess is that more than half the people in the ghetto were ill. Typhus fever was rampant. The lice were out of control and were eating holes through the dying bodies that littered the streets. I tried staying lice-free by bathing in freezing water, but avoiding the lice was next to impossible. Lice eggs covered my jacket. Dr. Kanizsai told me to keep washing my body with cold water and to stay as busy as possible to remain healthy and alive.

I was ready to give up and submit myself to death when I learned that, suddenly and miraculously, food was being provided to anyone who was willing to work. I knew I needed food. Even though I could barely walk, I decided to work. My duty was to clean the streets and tidy up the sleeping quarters of the Arrow Cross officers. The Arrow Cross militants also gave me a variety of other tasks. For my hard work, they gave me a cup of broth (which was really warm water). I wasn't satisfied, but I was glad that I at least had two warm liquids a day. Keeping myself physically active was also important because it kept me from freezing.

The Russian troops began advancing aggressively and were almost on the Pest side of Budapest. The chaotic conditions prevailed among the people. It seemed as though everyone wanted to go into hiding, including soldiers and officers in the Hungarian army. They no longer wanted to obey their new government's orders. They, too, had no more access to water, electricity, and food. Everyone was tired and fed up, and they wanted the war to end.

But the bad conditions turned into a Christmas nightmare. On Christmas Eve, the siege of Budapest began. Eichmann knew that the Russian troops had almost completed surrounding the boundaries of Budapest and that his stronghold was in jeopardy. He set forth his final command to the Nazi troops, ordering them to kill all the Jews in the Central Ghetto before evacuating Budapest. Naturally, none of us knew what was going on. I was barely surviving. On this evening, gunmen broke into a children's home, which was run by the International Red Cross. They shot some of the children and forced others to the banks of the Danube River, throwing them in to freeze and drown.

The rampage wasn't over. On Christmas Day, the Fascists broke into another children's home and shot the children, killing all but the girls. The young Jewish girls were spared from death, but they were assaulted, raped, and then tattooed as whores. After the girls suffered through that treatment, they endured additional violence from the Arrow Cross militants and Nazi gangs.[1] No one was safe. For the next couple of weeks, looting, rape, and murder became commonplace. Food and heat were still not available. When I wasn't doing my duties, I tried to make myself invisible.

By January 11, 1945, a plan was in motion to get rid of all of us Jews in the ghetto. We were to be bombed to death. The Arrow Cross Party began planting the bombs. We could not have escaped, even if we had known what was happening. The many escape fantasies I had entertained since entering the ghetto could not help me now.

Rumors were being spread that the Russians were coming and that, outside the ghetto, wall-to-wall fighting was in progress. Some hearing people told me they saw a couple of Russians peeking in through the ghetto fencing. I was trying to remain hopeful. For a solid week, I could see the fighting, the bullets flying through the air. I could feel the ground shaking tremendously.

On January 17, the Russians and Americans, independently, were fighting the Arrow Cross and Nazis soldiers on the outer perimeter of the ghetto area. They were closing in. The vibrations from the bombings become more frequent. At night, in the distance, I could see shots being fired that lit up the sky. I had no fear. I had no energy to be scared, and I figured that if a bomb came and I died, so what. I had lost interest in life. I was helpless—unable to move and without any freedom.

ON DEATH ROW

THE NEXT DAY, January 18, I awoke just before five o'clock in the morning. I noticed that the approximately thirty to thirty-five Arrow Cross officers were nowhere to be found. They had left the ghetto, knowing that the Russians were on their heels. I went outside to join hundreds of other souls to sit and die. Everybody was quiet. We had come to terms and had accepted our fate.

Out of nowhere, Russian soldiers began appearing in the ghetto. Each had a red star on his uniform. They were holding their guns pointed out in front of their bodies. The Jewish people, including myself, were on the ground in the middle of Klauzal Square. I got up to see what was happening. Dr. Kanizsai was talking to a Russian soldier. No more than two hours later, the Russians began hurrying us along, hollering that bombs were set to detonate by eight o'clock and that we were free to leave. We had less than an hour to clear out of the area.

I had been spared yet again. Everyone began hugging and crying and declaring, "Freedom from slavery!" The Russians had conquered Pest, though it wouldn't be until February 13 that the fighting in Buda would end.[1] January 18 would be the date of my death and rebirth, a day I would never forget.

Dr. Kanizsai gathered all of us together and said we were returning to the institute. I wanted to run as fast as I could to get out of the zone, but I could barely walk. All around me, people were scrambling to leave, though some were too weak to move and stayed right where they were. The journey back felt like an eternity. My feet were frostbitten, and my head was spinning.

We arrived at the institute relieved to see that the building was intact. The big problem was that all the storage supplies had been stripped. We had nothing to eat or drink. Dr. Kanizsai fervently began searching for aid—food, water, money, or whatever he could get. Everyone continued to scour the trash bins for food. I found some food that had to have been at least three to four months old, and I ate it. But it wasn't enough. My body was exhausted, malnourished, and frozen. At this point, I was very upset with the Russians. People in the ghetto had told me that the Communists were good, that they loved children, and that they would support us. But even though the Russians gave me my freedom, I was starving worse than ever. I began to believe that I was better off with the Arrow Cross troops because they had given me warm broth. I realized that, at this point, food was more important than freedom. I was not free from my physical needs. My mind was full of anguish. I no longer wanted to struggle and decided to let myself go. I felt as though I was in a dream.

That night, I lay down in a bed and went into a deep, deep sleep. I remained in a sleepy state for days, waking up occasionally to find myself shivering. The lice had infested my body, and the blood-eating bedbugs attacked me at night. I had no energy to pick them off, allowing them to enjoy my flesh and blood. Repeatedly, I dreamt about food and recalled my former days of picky eating. Half of me wanted to die, but the other half prayed for anything to improve.

Dr. Kanizsai was aware of my physical and mental state. A few more days passed, and he told me that I had to get out of bed to try and rebuild my strength. I told him I wanted to die. He continued to pressure me until I got out of bed. I felt like a walking icicle. When I went outside the building, I found Russian soldiers camping out. They had sacks of potatoes. I decided to sit beside them and collect the peels from their potatoes. I took the skins to the furnace in our building and roasted them to eat. They were crispy and delicious. For several weeks, I battled with Dr. Kanizsai to leave me alone and let me be. Every morning, he stood by my bedside until I put my feet on the ground and stood up.

Dr. Kanizsai finally received our badly needed aid. I received food and new clothing. Everyone had to strip naked and remove their sheets and blankets from their beds. Everything had to be boiled to kill the lice. For a long time afterward, the washing of our bedding and clothing continued to be a daily chore as we struggled to reduce the lice population. However, the bedbugs were very persistent. Dr. Kanizsai assigned another student to care for me because I was extremely weak. The student changed my bedding and made sure that I was eating.

Several weeks passed, and I began to regain my strength. Once Dr. Kanizsai saw that I was able to get out of bed on my own, he assigned me light cleaning duty. Several more weeks passed before my strength returned. Seeing my improved condition, Dr. Kanizsai gave me the responsibility of keeping the fire going in each classroom of the third and fourth floors. I had to chop wood with an ax and carry seventy pounds of coal, equal to my own body weight, from the basement to the top floors. I designed a strap that allowed me to carry the wicker basket filled with coals on my back. Two other boys who were both fifteen years old helped me. We were the only three who could manage the weight of the load. I was only eleven years old!

The Russian army battled almost three weeks to claim and liberate the entire side of Pest. They took even longer to seize the Buda side. The Nazi and Arrow Cross troops were retreating from the Pest side to the Buda side where they had established a strong presence. As the Nazi and Arrow Cross troops retreated from Pest, they planted bombs, which exploded all seven bridges connecting Buda to Pest. The collapsed bridges made it difficult for the Russian army to advance to Buda, but they eventually succeeded.

Although the Russians freed us from the ghetto, from one type of agony, the conditions remained far from good. The streets were piled high with rubble. Burnt vehicles littered the streets, and broken electrical wires dangled. Civilians, still suffering terribly, filled the streets. I remained skin and bones from the limited amount of food. The Russians did not supply us with any relief. And, even though Dr. Kanizsai provided us with food rations, they weren't enough. I continued searching the trash cans for additional food.

The Russian soldiers imposed their own brutality and ruthlessness. They actually continued on where the Nazi and Arrow Cross soldiers had left off, robbing the people of whatever remaining possessions they had. Drunken Russian soldiers set buildings ablaze and gang-raped vulnerable women. This turmoil would continue, especially after dark, for at least another year.

Clearly, by this time, most of the world knew what was happening. I wondered to myself how the world could just stand by and watch. The people's pleas for help were ignored. More perplexing was trying to figure out how groups of humans could murder other humans because of religion or race.

It took awhile for things to start settling down at the institute. Eventually, I got into a routine. Then, Dr. Kanizsai announced to us that a listing of survivors had been posted at the building of the Jewish headquarters. I wanted to know what had happened to my family. That day, I walked over to the building. I found only Lenke, Jolán, and Sándor's names on the list. My parents' names were missing, as were the names of Miklós, Salgo, Jenő, Magdalena, and Irén. I wished hard that they were still alive. I visited the headquarters weekly to see the updated listings but never saw any other of my family's names listed. Knowing that Lenke, Jolán, and Sándor were alive, I continually hoped that they would visit or contact me.

During the months of May and June, a Jewish American organization was instrumental in providing clothes, food, and medication to our institute. The organization was known as the American Jewish Joint Distribution Committee, which would continue providing us supplies until 1948. I called it "The Joint." If it weren't for their support, I may not be alive today. They provided us with everything, including canned milk, canned fruit, canned meat, peanuts, fruit, grapes, flour, clothing, blankets, medicine, cough syrup, vitamins, and even Hershey's chocolate candy bars. Three of us were assigned to pick up the food and supplies from the distribution center and deliver them to our institute.

The Joint also provided us with nurses. They made all of us take vitamins. Some of the children needed medication. I didn't. Children were still dying from diphtheria and a condition that gave them a yellow face. A lot of children had red rashes on their bodies. All kinds of diseases were present. The nurses provided care for the sick children and helped all of us children with our hygiene.

I was very skinny and my bones were showing. I was eleven years old and weighed about sixteen kilos (thirty-four pounds). I had a little abdominal swelling, but many of the children had more severe swelling because of starvation. As a result, many died. If their faces and arms swelled up, they would die. If the swelling confined itself to the stomach, they would usually recover. At the time, I thought the medicine was making them sick. I lost two friends from malnutrition. Both of them were originally from my hometown.

We had a room for sick people and a room for healthy people. Whenever I saw someone who looked really bad, I called the nurse over. She would do a checkup and report his or her condition to Dr. Kanizsai. Sometimes, I reported a child's condition to Dr. Kanizsai directly. The day after reporting one child to Dr. Kanizsai, I asked him about the status of the child. The child had died. I wasn't frightened to see death or to see any of my friends die. The ghetto had prepared me to face death.

Also during this time and into July, thousands of survivors began journeying back to Hungary and Poland in search of lost families.[2] Several of my siblings finally came to visit me. The first was my brother Salgo. I spotted him in the hall of the institute. I raced to him in total excitement and embraced him as hard as I could. I whimpered as he returned the embrace. He looked very thin and his eyes were bugged out. He could produce only a little smile with his suffering face. My mind reeled with questions. I told him I had been so worried about him because his name was not posted on the survivor's list.

We didn't talk much, but he briefly explained his ordeal in a hard-labor camp. He had just come from a hospital, which one, I don't know. He gave me brief details about how our farm home had been pillaged by the Fascists. He had come by to see me because he wanted me to know he was on his way back home to Komjat. He felt there was nowhere else for him to go. He wanted to see what was left, determine what he could salvage, and decide whether it was worthwhile to start over. I begged him to take me with him. When he said he couldn't, I made him promise to keep in touch.

A few weeks later, my sister Lenke came to visit. I knew she had survived, but I did not know she would visit me. I was in the hallway and spotted her at the entrance. We hugged tightly and both cried continuously. I still cry when I think of seeing her at that moment. She looked well. Her good condition must have resulted from the food and medication that the Americans had provided to her. She was thin, but the coloring in her face looked good. She had been in Auschwitz. She gave me the dreaded news I did not want to hear— that my parents and younger brother Jenő had been killed. Lenke continued to tell me about my parents. My father had become very sick. Lenke thought something was wrong with his kidneys. Apparently, he did have some kidney problems before the war. She was unsure about how my mother and Jenő died. Much later, I learned from Péter that his mother told him my mother had died in the gas shower. Lenke also knew that our oldest brother Miklós had died. She had heard rumors that he had been forced to dig his own grave and was then shot next to it. I asked her about Jolán. Lenke said, "She's alive in Germany. She is planning to go back to Komjat." She added that Sándor was also alive and that Irén and Magdalena were very sick. The Swedish Red Cross had taken both of them to Sweden for treatment because they had tuberculosis.

Then, she cried and begged my forgiveness, blaming herself for my being deaf. She offered no details, just penance. I realized that she had been only ten years old when I was one year old—only a child herself. The memory of that incident and its consequences had been a tremendous burden for her to carry, a calamity for which she never forgave herself. I tried to comfort her, telling her not to worry. She stayed with me for about an hour. She was planning to return to Komjat. She could not take me back home but promised to keep in touch. I am sure both Salgo and Lenke knew I had no future in Komjat—like my parents did.

Weeks went by, and Jolán finally came to visit. She was on the thin side but was dressed well. She brought along her new husband, Aron.

Jolán embraced me lovingly, just as Salgo and Lenke had done. Jolán explained that she had been in Auschwitz and had gone home to visit with Salgo and Lenke. She felt that the farm was no longer her home and wanted a new life. She told me that, eventually, she and Aron were planning to move to America. But first, they were moving to Germany.

I begged her to take me along. I complained to her about Dr. Kanizsai treating me as his personal slave. After our approximately hour-and-one-half visit, Jolán went to Dr. Kanizsai about my complaints. Jolán had no intentions of taking me with her, and after she went to Dr. Kanizsai, my relationship with him grew more difficult. She spoke with him for about half an hour and came back telling me I had to stay. I begged her again to take me. Instead, she promised to send gifts and supplies as well as to make all the necessary arrangements for me to join her in America. I believed her. I was a child. Jolán was my godmother. Unfortunately, she never kept her promise, leaving a deep wound in my heart.

My last visitor was my brother, Sándor. I was especially excited to see him because I had looked up to him as my protector. His face and body looked healthy. I believe Sándor was the lucky one of the family. The Nazis favored him somewhat because he could speak German. He became the interpreter for everybody. They gave him comfortable sleeping quarters, food, and other basics. He was a tall boy. I think if he had been short, the Nazis would have gassed him.

We began reminiscing about our time on the farm. Sándor had been my protector, always there for me in any situation. We recalled a particular situation when a farm boy continuously teased me. Sándor had me point out the boy to him and then went after him to beat him. The boy's parents complained to the farm police. When the farm police showed up at our farm with the neighbor's complaint, my mother was the one to intervene and explain the situation. My mother had a way with words, and she convinced the police that I had been teased and that my brother Sándor had protected me in defense. The farm police respected my mother and let the circumstance go unpunished.

I mentioned that even though Sándor was my protector, we also fought a lot. He laughed and told me that he had allowed me to win so I would feel good. I shared with Sándor that I had felt sorry for him because he had suffered so much while under the strict teachings of my father, especially, those times that my father whipped his fingers with a wooden stick when Sándor didn't follow the Hebrew words correctly. My heart now understood Sándor's experience.

Sándor had no intention or desire to go back to Komjat and had already made plans to move to Italy. I begged him to take me along with him. But he said I couldn't go, and I began to cry. When it was time for him to leave, I chased after him. On the street, we happened to run into Dr. Kanizsai. Sándor's Hungarian wasn't very good, so he asked Dr. Kanizsai if he could speak German. Lucky for Sándor, Dr. Kanizsai could speak German. Obviously, I couldn't understand what was being said, and Dr. Kanizsai was not interpreting. Afterward, Sándor looked at me and said he would write a letter as soon as he arrived in Italy. As I look back now, I realize Sándor had been only fourteen years old then—a youngster. Dr. Kanizsai tried to comfort me and, at the same time, told me that I was to remain at the institute.

Approximately a year and a half had passed since I had last seen my family. Now I felt a renewed sense of loss. The connection with my family would forever be a broken puzzle even though some of them were still alive. I prayed that they would keep their promises about updating me with news by means of letters and packages. Their promises were my only hope and comfort.

After seeing Sándor, I had to accept my status as an orphan. I realized that my brothers and sisters were also orphans. In our visits, none of us shared with each other the details of our experiences during the Holocaust. I don't know if my siblings shared among themselves, but they never shared their feelings with me. I didn't share either. We simply didn't ask one another. After having endured that pain, what was the sense of rehashing those memories at that time?

Shortly after Sándor's visit, I received from my sisters Magdalena and Irén a letter and package containing candies, figs, nuts, cookies, and soap. Magdalena had shortened her name to Magda. The communication came to me by way of the Swedish Red Cross because the regular mail was still out of commission. They wrote about being in Auschwitz. After their camp was liberated, the Red Cross medics had diagnosed both of them with tuberculosis. They were sent to a sanitarium to heal, and the Swedish government provided all their health care. I was overcome with happiness, knowing they were alive and safe in Sweden. Later, I learned that Irén had only the beginning stages of tuberculosis, and her health quickly improved. Magdalena's case was more advanced, but she, too, eventually healed. At the sanitarium, Magdalena met her future husband Meir, who had a more advanced case of tuberculosis.

I was now relieved to know where all my siblings were and what their plans for the short-term future would be. Then, bringing yet more relief, another live soul came back to the institute to join us— Sándor Weicker. He had survived Mauthausen Camp. But the horrors weren't completely over. Atrocities continued, and the accounts of others would continue to haunt us.

Knowing that summer was coming to an end and school would resume again, I decided to take a stroll through the city park. It was a beautiful, warm day. I was admiring my surroundings when I noticed some bushes shaking. I saw a Russian soldier struggling with a young Hungarian girl. I decided to get a closer look and hid behind a tree. I watched as the soldier pushed the girl to the ground and proceeded to rape her. I knew that my interference could get me killed. I could do nothing to help her. I was nauseated by the soldier's actions. I felt the shame and hurt that the girl was experiencing.

Later, on one of the final days of the summer, I met up with a man I had known before the war. We warmly greeted each other. But as he began speaking, I noticed that he had few teeth. Before the war, he had had the straightest, most beautiful teeth. I asked him what happened. He went into gross detail about his days of hiding and his survival technique of posing as a non-Jew. He even had fake identification. However, he blew his cover one day when he happened to be urinating in a public restroom and an Arrow Cross officer came in. The Arrow Cross officer looked over at him and noticed that he was circumcised, which meant he was a Jew. The Arrow Cross officer used his brass knuckles and beat my friend's face. That was why he had sixteen missing teeth.

But what truly appalled me were his detailed accounts of the Arrow Cross militants' killing for sport. Sometimes, they used their German shepherd dogs to chase down and attack a person. Once the dog successfully pinned the person down to the ground, the officer would then beat the person to a pulp. At other times, they beat a person and then drowned the victim in a latrine. Apparently, babies were the best because the officers would try to flush the whole body. In other instances, they stripped the Jewish girls and women of their clothes, raped and beat them, then tied them by their ankles with rope and reeled them down headfirst into a well to drown. I was truly sickened by the accounts at that point and told the toothless man I had heard enough.

I wondered whether the man must have felt helpless, watching other Jews suffer. He may have felt guilty for posing as a non-Jew. I wondered, but I never asked him. In any event, this toothless man was not saddened that his teeth had been knocked out. He was happy to be alive, especially after all that he had witnessed.

The man's story prompted me to remember all the newspaper article discussions on what to do with the Jews. I had never understood how Jews could be labeled subhuman. In fact, I saw all humans as equals, each person being responsible for his or her own actions. However, after being at the hands of the Arrow Cross Party, after losing my family members, and after listening to this toothless man, I was sure that the Fascists were subhuman.

CHAPTER 10 (1945–1948)

THE BAR MITZVAH AND ZIONISM

IN THE FALL of 1945, the institute had to go through an overhaul. Many repairs were needed, and the filth was atrocious. The cleanup would take months. All of the institute's supplies had been depleted.

Márkus Kohn, Hermann Zoldán, Ernö Rosenblüth, and I continued with our duties. The four of us were responsible for picking up food from the Joint and delivering it to our institute. Dr. Kanizsai gave us plenty of other duties, too. In addition, I was still responsible for preparing wood for the furnace to keep the rooms heated. I had become a workhorse.

After the winter break, classes resumed. I attended school halftime, so my duties were cut in half. Nobody had to pay at the time; the school was free. Péter had returned to the institute, and he shared his traumatic experience. He was lucky though because his mother was still alive. Sári néni returned to the institute as an instructor. She was very happy to see me because we hadn't seen each other since she left me at the Red Cross. I continued with my duties at the institute. When my daily chores were completed, I attended classes. I was now in the fourth grade.

Things held steady throughout the winter. A year had already gone by since I had waited for a letter from my mother. Everyday, I thought of my family, wishing they would come for me. I had to be strong like a man and not show my emotions. Besides, I felt different now; I had grown and had to present myself as being more independent.

Around this time, Szálasi got what he had coming, which was politically pleasing to me. American soldiers arrested him in Austria. They found King Stephen's crown and a gold hand in a trunk that he possessed. The Americans confiscated the items. Szálasi was sent to the Budapest jail where he awaited his trial. Later, the court found him guilty of his crimes and ordered him to hang. The people were elated with the outcome. When the hanging was complete, the people in the city of Budapest celebrated.

In the summer, we orphans continued to live at the institute. Our only requirement was to be in by eight o'clock in the evening. The students who were not orphans went home to their families. Because Péter was not an orphan, he was able to attend only daytime classes and go home to his mother in the evenings and on the weekends. At least I got to see him during the day. I was envious of him; however, staying at the institute wasn't all bad because we were free to do as we pleased.

The summer was full of unstructured time, and I went to the circus and movies frequently. All of the excursions were free to anyone who was deaf. I also relaxed at the institute with my friends, often going to a man-made lake close by. The water was filthy and swimming in it was illegal, but I swam anyway. I found the water to be soothing.

I also began attending a Bible study class, which was held four hours each week.[1] A new boy named Pál Löwenstein entered the institute. Prior to the war, Pál had attended one of the largest Hungarian deaf schools in Budapest, established in 1802. It was a government school, not a Jewish school. Pál and I were the same age. His father introduced us to each other and told me, "You two will be good friends and you need to help each other." I agreed. From that point on, Pál became my best friend. I taught him chess and table tennis.

During the fall, I received a letter from Lenke. She complained of the struggles at home in Komjat and explained that she would be unable to care for me. I shared the letter with the nurse at the institute because I couldn't fully comprehend Lenke's writing. As I watched the nurse read the letter, she began to cry. The nurse explained that Lenke and Salgo were living together at my home in Komjat and that Lenke was in a helpless situation. They were barely surviving. I was sad about the circumstances, and I felt that, if I were there, I could help. I also wanted to be at home with a part of my family. But because of the border blockage between the countries, I was unable to respond. Czechoslovákia was now part of Russia, and no mail was permitted to go through, which left me frustrated. We wouldn't be able to communicate with each other again until 1956.

Then, György Weltner came to visit me. I hadn't seen him since our days in the Red Cross camp more than a year before. György told me that, after the Red Cross, he had gone back home to find his father alive. Unfortunately, his mother died in the Bergen-Belsen

Hermann Zoldán and I after swimming.

Pál Löwenstein is the second from the right and I am sitting next to him on the left. Ernö Rosenblüth is on the far left and Hermann Zoldán is on the far right.

camp. György was not a student at the institute. He was a good friend of Sándor Weicker, and joined us regularly to play soccer. György, Pál, and I became close friends.

Although my friendships had improved, I felt that my existence had become extremely mundane. I was no longer happy with my school and felt like Dr. Kanizsai was using me as his workhorse. I fought with him constantly about various matters and was fed up with him. One day, after a fight, Dr. Kanizsai gave me a punishment. I fled from the institute. I remembered Weicker and Striker, who got in trouble for reporting Dr. Kanizsai. I didn't care. I was willing to face the consequences.

I went to see Margit at her home. She had been my counselor at our institute, but she was now working for the Zionist Organization. Margit was surprised to see me and invited me in. I told her about

Dr. Kanizsai treating me like his slave and begged her to let me stay with her. She was very receptive and sensitive and had a way of understanding my feelings. Plus, she did not get along with Dr. Kanizsai either. In fact, she told me, he was the reason she had left the institute. We talked until very late, and she suggested that I spend the night. I shared the bed with her while she comforted me.

The following morning, Margit told me she was now working for the Zionist Organization. She told me that the Zionist Organization was similar to the Jewish community and that the group was playing an instrumental role in helping Jewish people relocate to Palestine. I decided to join. She asked whether I was interested in moving to Palestine. I wanted to go, and she approved. She told me that I would be joining a group of children from my institute who were planning to go.

I stayed with her at work to learn more about the organization. Margit gave me a Zionist pin to wear, saying that I was now an official member. She instructed me that I should no longer say hello in the Hungarian language. My new word for hello would now be "Shalom." She told me stories of how fantastic Palestine was and what a wonderful life I would soon have.

Later that day, Margit contacted Sári néni. Margit needed Sári néni to be her liaison to Dr. Kanizsai because Margit needed his approval to release me into her care along with a group of other students from the institute who also wanted to move to Palestine. Margit believed that Sári néni was the only person who could persuade Dr. Kanizsai to approve the move.

Sári néni discussed the plan with Dr. Kanizsai, and he reluctantly approved the move. However, in exchange, I would have to stay at the institute until the time came to leave, which would be at the end of the school year in June. I felt uncomfortable and angry to go back, but I agreed to the arrangement. Margit accompanied me back to the institute. Naturally, Dr. Kanizsai had nothing negative to say because he needed me to do his dirty work. During my time off from work and school, I spent quite a bit of time with Margit, sometimes spending the night with her. She was a real comfort.

By Hanukkah, I was able to recite the holiday prayers. I was also fortunate enough to receive a Hanukkah gift from the Joint. By this time, I had become a devout Zionist member. I proudly wore my Zionist pin, which declared "Zionist Power, Group Power."

Spring was a very busy time. For my thirteenth birthday, I received a chessboard from Sári néni. I was excited and wanted to get more involved with chess. I bought myself a chess book and immediately began improving. My goal was to become a good chess player.

During this time, my relationship with one of the counselors, Árpád, grew closer. Árpád was also Dr. Kanizsai's secretary. He had depended on my help since the first day I entered the institute. I didn't mind doing chores or errands for him. I shared with him my frustrations about Dr. Kanizsai. He always expressed his love and his trust of me. He suggested I do more for him, which meant that I would do less for Dr. Kanizsai. Árpád told Dr. Kanizsai he needed extra help and suggested me as a helper. Dr. Kanizsai agreed. Under Árpád's command, I ran errands to the post office and delivered letters and Joint supplies. Sometimes I did light office work. Once a week, I delivered food and money to his mother, who tipped me and gave me hugs.

Árpád also gave me a new chore. I had to assist a blind boy, named Ödon Bokor by dropping him off and picking him up daily at the blind school. Árpád paid me for that duty at the end of each week. Ödon and I were the same age. We should have been bar mitzvahed around the same time. Ödon decided to go through the bar mitzvah process, and I chose not to. When Ödon was finally bar mitzvahed, I was disappointed that he didn't invite me to the ceremony. After the bar mitzvah, he showed me his many gifts. I wished I could have the pocket watch, money, and new clothes he had received. My envy was intense.

During the interim, I was unaware that my Bible teacher, Ábrahám Benedek, had been in search of my father's brother. Ábrahám wanted my uncle to sponsor my bar mitzvah training. Ábrahám was successful at locating my uncle, and my uncle was willing to help out. My uncle came to visit me and encouraged me to change my mind and pursue the bar mitzvah process. At first, I thought of Ödon's fantastic gifts, but then I realized that my feelings were more important than the gifts. I told my uncle I was not interested in being bar mitzvahed, and he was appalled by my resistance. He wanted to know why, but I refused to give him an answer. Besides, I didn't care what he thought. I was mad and felt betrayed by him. I knew that, because I was deaf, he had no real interest in me. He had never bothered to find me after the war. He came forward only at the request of Ábrahám.

I had serious reasons for not going through the bar mitzvah process. I was sincerely confused by the communistic rule and influence. The communist belief insisted that God did not exist, yet I was attending religious classes, which spoke of God. Did He exist or not? I vividly recalled praying to God from morning to night in the ghetto and wondering, if there is a God, where is He and how could He allow so many people to suffer and perish? After recalling the survivor's list and my conversation with Lenke, I again wondered, if there is a God, why did He take my parents and brothers away?

After considering my circumstances and what I had experienced, I decided for two reasons that it was best to believe there was no God. First, if I did not agree outwardly with the Communists, I could suffer socially, which could alienate me from possible future endeavors within my country. Second, I vividly recalled my father's prayers every Saturday and my own prayers in the ghetto, none of which had prevented my pain and suffering. Nevertheless, I decided to continue with my religious classes out of pure interest. I was now also able to recite the seder prayers in Hebrew.

In the midst of all that was happening, Dr. Kanizsai gave me another responsibility. At first, I was angry that he was giving me something else to do, until he told me what I'd actually be doing. I was to take József Weissz to visit his aunt and cousins on the weekends. Dr. Kanizsai felt that József was too young to make the trip alone. It made me feel good that I was the one who made it possible for József to see his family. József had lost his parents and other family members in the Holocaust. His aunt and cousins were the last of his existing family whom he could visit. The weekends with József were enjoyable. His aunt spoiled us rotten. They liked me very much and always told me that I was a good boy. They gave József and I an equal allowance. Anything they gave to József, they gave to me. His aunt had a good heart. She even bought and donated a Ping-Pong table to the institute.

Spring was coming to an end. I was glad, because now I could move to Palestine. Our Zionist group was filled with excitement. We had daily discussions about our move and our future in a strange and new place. We had only a few weeks until it was time to go.

Then came that dreadful day when Dr. Kanizsai changed his mind about letting us go. His reasons were unclear. I figured that, if he released us, then he wouldn't have a job—period! Sári néni quit the institute immediately and became his worst enemy. Dr. Kanizsai was a selfish man, fulfilling his own needs whenever he could. I felt as though he had manipulated us. The institute was required to maintain a student quota to keep its doors open. If we all left, the institute could not meet its quota. I, along with the rest of the group, felt devastated. His decision was a huge disappointment. The parents and families of four students pulled them out of the institute and sent them to Palestine.

I also believe that Dr. Kanizsai was a greedy man. Many years after I became an adult, Magda told me that while she and Irén were living in Sweden, they regularly had sent packages to the institute. I was shocked because I had received only two packages the entire time. I am sure Dr. Kanizsai kept the packages for himself. My belief is based on the fact that all packages arriving at the institute went directly to Dr. Kanizsai's office for review and, supposedly, distribution. I believe my theory is correct. He was a powerful man. He could take what he wanted. I was nothing.

Sári néni was so disappointed with Dr. Kanizsai that she decided to quit teaching at the institute. Not being able to move to Palestine was devastating enough. Now, losing Sári néni left a gaping hole in my heart. I would no longer be able to see her on a daily basis. She tried to comfort me, assuring me that I could visit her whenever possible.

Sári néni's immediate replacement was József Simon. He was another excellent teacher and had been the chief educator at nine deaf schools in Hungary prior to World War II. He had gone from school to school conducting inspections. He was also an evangelical priest who taught religion classes. After the war, most of the Jewish teachers had been killed. Only two were left. In addition, the school was no longer an exclusively Jewish school but now also had Christian students. Thus, József was a great choice. However, József was more than a teacher and priest. He was a kind man. He taught us how to plant a vegetable garden and, later, how to stake tomatoes and bell peppers. He also taught us how to plant trees. Before the war, we rarely went outside to play at the institute, but József had us go out and play soccer. We even played on a swing. Occasionally, he would take some of us to the movies.

One such movie that will remain forever in my mind was about an Italian orphan boy whose wealthy parents had left him to be raised by a Catholic bishop after their deaths. When the boy turned ten, the bishop had to leave for South America but decided it was best for the boy to remain in Italy under another bishop's care.

The second bishop raised him and sent him off to college. While in college, the young man became involved with the Italian struggle against the Austrian occupation and was elected as the student organization's leader. Still, he remained confused over whether or not he was doing the right thing. At Easter, he went to confession and revealed his actions to a priest. The priest then asked him for his name and the names of his fellow revolutionaries. The next morning, both he and all the people he mentioned in his confession were arrested. Realizing he had been betrayed by the priest, he returned to his home at the church after his release and tore down all the crosses and everything else that referenced God. He then embraced communism and left Italy for South America to help spread the movement's ideas.

When he later returned to Italy, he was quickly arrested by the Austrians, declared a traitor, and sentenced to death in front of a firing squad. When the original bishop, who had become a powerful

Our class photo from 1947. I'm at the far left in front of József Simon.

cardinal, returned to Italy and learned of the young man's fate, he became determined to get the young man out of jail. He met with the Austrian commander and bribed him with a large sum of money to fake the execution.

When the day of the young man's execution arrived, the firing squad was ordered to fire their guns but not to aim at the prisoner. Unfortunately, the young man had not been told of the cardinal's arrangement with the commander. After the firing squad shot at him, and the young man realized he had not been hit, he began to taunt the squad, until one officer took aim, shot, and killed him.

The cardinal watched helplessly as the young man fell to the ground dead. He ran out of the building, held the young man in his arms, and cried "My son, where is God?"

I was moved by this movie, and couldn't stop crying. How could I believe in God now? I had cried out to God in the ghetto. I had cried out to God for my parents and siblings. Watching the cardinal cry out only confirmed my disbelief in God that much more. I began to reason that communism could be the answer.

By summertime, 1947, I was visiting Sári néni's Uncle and Aunt Balkányi every Saturday. I traveled to their home and back to the institute by means of bus and trolley car. Each week, I got to their home in the early afternoon and stayed for dinner. They considered me to be part of their family and enjoyed having my company. I really liked them, too. During my visits, they provided me with a weekly allowance, which was a real treat for me.

By this time, my errands and duties at the institute had dwindled to almost nothing. I wanted more pocket change. Dr. Kanizsai and other staff members gave me duties, and I made sure not to complain about what they were giving me. The deliveries were especially worth doing because I received pay from the institute's staff in addition to tips at my delivery stops. With my tip money, I could afford to do things such as eat ice cream and go out on small outings.

The fall months flew by, and on December 5, all of us children were told to polish and shine our shoes, then put them in our bedroom windows.[2] I thought the request was quite odd. We were told that if we followed these instructions, Santa Claus would come. We all believed it. The following morning, I went downstairs and found Santa Claus handing out candies and gifts to all the children. However, Hanukkah came without gifts from the Joint. The only memorable event during Hanukkah was reciting my prayers on the first night of the holiday.

In the following months, we observed other important Jewish occasions. By March, I was given an acting role for the Purim play and enjoyed performing. A month later, I again recited the prayers in Hebrew at the Passover seder for which Dr. Kanizsai and I were the leaders.

Then, in May, József took us to the circus. I was amazed. A French man lay down with boards placed across his chest. Then, a horse walked on him. I couldn't believe that the French man didn't get crushed. Equally astonishing was the man who lay on a bed of nails. Concrete blocks were placed on his chest, and two men with sledgehammers broke the blocks. When the man rose to his feet, his back was unscathed. Only slight red pinpricks were visible.

We also saw a circus man who had a way with numbers. He asked the audience to give him a math calculation. A man in the audience rose to his feet and said, "three hundred fifty-eight multiplied by seven hundred twenty-eight," and sat back down. The incredible circus man stood silent and thought carefully, then gave his response. The man in the audience again stood up and declared, "You are wrong." The circus man rethought the equation. He realized his error, and gave the correct response. The man in the audience clapped his hands and sat back down. The audience cheered. I looked over at József and could tell by the expression on his face that he was truly impressed.

The end of spring brought another letter from Magda and Irén as well as a letter and fantastic package from Sándor, who was still in Italy. Sándor's package contained delicious oranges and figs.

CHAPTER **11** (1948–1949)

A SUMMER VACATION AND A KISS

SUMMERTIME HAD come again, and József decided that Hermann, Ernö, and I would accompany him on a one-month vacation. Leaving Budapest by train, we traveled to the city of Eger, located between the Mátra and Bükk mountains in northeastern Hungary. We stayed at a deaf school in Eger where we were provided with a room and meals. The principal of the school invited us to be his guests for dinner. The principal was a good friend of József's and, therefore, treated us like family. I wasn't at all homesick for my institute and, in fact, was happy to be out.

Each day in Eger was enjoyable. Daily, we swam at the public swimming pool and went sightseeing. Eger's varied architecture and its turbulent history fascinated me. It had a tremendous Turkish ambiance. We visited a huge Turkish mausoleum and learned that the city had been controlled by the Turks for nearly 150 years.

We were told a very interesting legend about how the women of Eger freed their husbands from the Turks. It so happened that the Turkish forces had moved into Eger. They stole everyone's land and made the men of Eger their slaves. The women of Eger feared for their lives and went into hiding in the mountains where they single-handedly conjured up a plan to oust the Turkish forces. They boiled water for days and then dumped barrelsful down the mountain, creating a mudslide. The mudslide destroyed the Turkish forces, and the ones who survived fled. The women of Eger regained control, getting back their land and their men. The story may have been a myth, but I believed it.

After three weeks in the fascinating city of Eger, we traveled to the city of Debrecen, the second largest city in Hungary. Again, we stayed at a deaf school, which provided us with a room and meals. Here, too, the principal of the school was a friend of József's. Once again, we shared dinner with the principal, who treated us like family.

Debrecen also had its charm and fascination. The area of the city had been inhabited since the Stone Age, and it, too, had a Turkish influence. During the Turkish wars, Debrecen was considered a border town and was able to keep its autonomy. Scythian and Avar tribes had lived there in historical times. Although Debrecen had been saturated by invaders throughout its history, the people of Debrecen had always been considered "free citizens." It was a center of trade and culture. After one week of sightseeing, we ventured back to Eger for a one-day stay before boarding the train back to Budapest.

At the train station in Eger, waiting to leave for Budapest, I stumbled upon a beautiful pear tree, loaded with fruit. I began picking the pears, eating one after another. I ate so many that within an hour, I was in tremendous pain. I went to Jozsef, and told him of my stomach pain.

He took me to the bar at the station, and ordered a half a deciliter of apricot brandy. He took the first swig and insisted I finish it off. The pain diminished almost instantly. After that, my stomach felt much better. Then, we all boarded the train back to Budapest.

When we returned to the institute, I continued my summer adventure. In the school yard, I played hide-and-go-seek with my friends. On one occasion, I ran behind a tree but found no room to hide. A girl was already hiding there. I had no time left to find another hiding place. In an effort to share the space, I pressed my body against hers so I wouldn't be seen. At once, I felt a rush of excitement surge through my body, a sensation that seemed familiar. The feeling sparked a memory of a dream I had had about seeing four nude girls. The dream had been exciting; now, that feeling had returned, and I was awake!

Apparently, our feelings were mutual, and the girl instantly motioned me to follow her down to the former bomb shelter. She took off her underwear in the dark and grabbed my hand. I didn't know how or what I was supposed to do with either her or myself. We explored each other's private parts for awhile, and I experienced my first kiss on the lips. From that point on, I began paying attention to girls.

At the end of the summer, before school resumed its sessions, I became ill with the flu. I was sent to the infirmary, where all sick children were required to go. While I was in bed, a fifteen-year-old girl, Eva, who liked me, sneaked into the infirmary. I was asleep and awoke to her kissing me. She motioned me to follow her into an empty armoire, and we kissed for hours. We shared many kissing sessions in the armoire. We usually met when we knew the other children had been dismissed to play outside.

Fall returned, and we learned that the Communists had won in the Parliamentary elections. The Hungarian government had officially become a Communist government. As a result, the Communist Hungarian Communist government now controlled the institute. They immediately converted the institute from a school for Jewish and Christian children to a government school. In addition, the Joint was cut off as a source of aid because the school was now under government control.

I remained at the school even though it had changed hands. Under Communist rule, all children were required to attend school. I was required to attend on a full-time basis. Students were not allowed to work. By request and in secret, I was given permission to continue doing light office work and deliveries on a part-time basis. I was relieved because I could continue receiving tips from my deliveries.

I was now in the seventh grade. Even though the school was under Communist rule, all children were required to continue to receive biblical training according to their denomination. Naturally, the parents made the final choice whether or not they wanted their child to receive the training. Because I was an orphan, I was asked directly whether or not I wished to receive the training. I decided to continue my training with Ábrahám, who had become a member of the Communist Party. I appreciated that he had never pushed me into the bar mitzvah process.

By winter, a new form of currency called the *forint* was established. The economy was improving, and the people seemed to have improved their lifestyle. People were being treated more equally. Naturally, we had our December 5 Santa Claus ritual again, and I continued reciting the Hanukkah prayers, without the celebration.

Sometime during the early part of spring, I received a letter from Irén saying she was moving to California, where Jolán and her family were now residing. I felt resentful because she didn't ask me whether I wanted to come along. Jolán had broken her promise by not sending for me. I didn't bother to respond to her letter. I knew it would be a waste of my time.

When seventh grade ended in June, Dr. Kanizsai grew concerned about what to do with me. The school did not offer an eighth-grade class, and I was ready to advance. Most of my friends and a handful of other students had either quit school or had transferred by this point. Dr. Kanizsai's solution was to search for another deaf school in Budapest that also provided housing. Péter was able to transfer to a school in Budapest for hard of hearing students. The school did not have a dormitory, but that was all right because he had a place to live. Meanwhile, most children at the institute were sent home for the summer. I had to swallow hard at the fact that I had to remain at school for the summer months.

CHAPTER **12** (1949–1950)

FOUND: A GOVERNMENT SCHOOL, BUT NO GOD

BY THE FALL of 1949, Dr. Kanizsai had found me another deaf school, a government school with a dormitory. I entered the eighth grade.

The communication among the deaf students at the government school was similar to the communication at the institute. Some signs were different, especially the numbers. For example, at my new school, the sign for the number twenty was made by sticking the thumb and forefinger out with the palm facing the ground. At the institute, the number twenty was signed by drawing the forefinger behind the ear. Luckily, we all were used to the oral method of communicating, so by relying on oral methods with the hand signals attached, we easily figured out one another's signs.

My new school provided me with the opportunity to continue with my Bible studies. I was beginning to learn the historical aspects of the Bible, which I found to be fascinating. Because of my interest, I began to question the Communist belief system. However, I was still not sure about the possibility of a God.

My new principal was Pál Györfi. He had brown hair, was of medium height, and had a stocky build. He seemed to be good-natured but strict at the same time. The school also employed two deaf teachers. He told me I would have a woman teacher named Zelky Gustavne. The *ne* at the end of her Hungarian name signified that she was a married woman and that her husband's name was Gustav. I was surprised to see Mrs. Gustavne. She had been the vice principal at my former institute at one time. She was slim and about five feet, five inches tall. Her brown hair was highlighted by gray, and she wore it curled up at the back of her head.

Having gotten special permission from Pál to leave the school grounds on the weekends, I socialized at the deaf club in the com-

munity, went to the movies, and played table tennis and cards. I
also became a member of the deaf club chess team, setting aside my
Sundays for tournament play. Our chess team competed against the
chess teams of the various hearing clubs.

During my Saturday visit to Aunt and Uncle Balkányi, I was taken
aback when they announced to me that it would be the last time I
would see them. They were moving to England. Sári néni's parents
had already moved to Paris, France. Uncle Balkányi knew the Communist Party would win; he sold everything and quickly left the
country.

After class on school days, we children went upstairs to the
study room. During this time, I practiced my chess game for the
weekend tournaments. The study room was also a good time to talk
about politics and many other subjects. Some of the younger children sat around to observe the conversations of us older students.
Several of the teens would tell the younger children to get lost or
would call them names. I always stepped in, telling them to allow
the younger children to observe. I believed that the younger children could learn from the older ones because I had benefited
greatly at my former institute by watching the counselors bicker
and argue over politics. There, we young children had always been
included as part of the group, and our exposure to adults had enabled us to learn. I tried to impress this philosophy on the older
children of my new school.

Here at this new school, I was more active than I had been at my
former institute. The government school had more to offer and had
better quality programs, including an excellent gymnastic program
and team. I wanted to join the team, but I had minimal experience,
so I struggled to master the basics in the gymnastics program.

The downfall of my new school was the anti-Semitism that lingered among the students. They knew I was a Jew. Only one other
Jewish student attended the school, but he didn't live in the dorms
like I did. Most likely, other Jewish children also attended; however,
many students refused to proclaim their religious beliefs and back-

At a public pool in Budapest with friends from the government school. From left to right, István Szabo, me, György Herbszt, Sándor Kiss, Géza Kukucska. The girl in front is Szidi Koszta.

ground. They were frightened. In any event, I felt as though I had no brotherhood and longed for companionship.

Outside the walls of our school, the communist politics began to shift. The Communist and Social Democratic parties joined forces to become the Labor Party. Because of the merger, two-thirds of the Parliament now represented the Labor Party, thus, squeezing out the smaller parties such as the Farm Party.

During the fall season, I was given a duty to create decorative propaganda that favored communism. The banners and painted signs I made read, "Viva Stalin," and I hung them throughout the school. Pál was extremely satisfied with my work and decorations. He felt sorry for me because the government was not providing me with any clothing or support. To show his appreciation for my efforts, he bought me a new pair of shoes.

By December, I had made several friends and considered myself popular. One morning, some of my friends asked me about my religious beliefs. I had never shared my thoughts of religion in the past because I was leery of the consequences. I was also still sorting out my feelings about God, my interest in the Bible, and the appealing logic of communism. However, I figured it was safe to speak outwardly about my fledgling communist belief because these students were attending a Communist government school. By now, I figured they were probably all Communists, with the exception of the one Jewish boy. I decided to tell them that I didn't believe God existed. After I said it, they all looked shocked. I didn't know it at the time, but they went directly to their Catholic priest to report what I had innocently proclaimed. The priest, in turn, went to Pál and complained about what I had said. That afternoon, Pál called me into his office. The sunlight in his office made the room exceptionally warm. I was already a bit anxious about being summoned into Pál's office, and in the already warm room, I began perspiring profusely. Pál questioned me about why I would make a statement that God did not exist to the other students. I explained that everyone should follow the communist belief system. I went on to tell Pál that my parents had prayed to God daily and they were killed, so there must not be a God. I also told him about the bishop in the Italian movie I had seen, angrily wondering where God was after the boy, his charge, was killed. Pál was unable to respond, but he wasn't angry with me.

Later on that evening, after dinner, I went up to my room for the night. Laszlo, my counselor, came in to see me a couple of hours later. He brought up the incident about what I had shared with the other children, including my discussion with Pál. We argued constructively into the wee hours of the morning about who created the earth, whether or not God existed, evolution, and so forth. During our intense evening discussion, we found time to fit in a few chess games. He made me promise him that I would no longer tell others that God did not exist.

The next day happened to be my Bible study class. Ábrahám had also learned of the incident. He took me off to the side and gave me a long lecture. He couldn't understand why I would say God was nonexistent, especially when I was continuing with my Bible studies. I told him that he had no business teaching me about Judaism because he was a Communist Party member and that Communists

didn't believe in God. He was shocked by my words and listened to
me as I rambled on. I told him that if we were to continue meeting,
then we should discuss politics rather than religion. He actually
agreed. And from that day forward, in secret, we omitted biblical
studies and focused on politics. We became good friends, and he was
happy he could keep his job.

A few days later, some of the students insulted me by calling me a
Jew in a derogatory way. I lashed out by punching and beating them.
I couldn't handle being singled out in such a negative way. From that
point on, I fought anyone who mouthed the word *Jew* in my face.
I even tried using karate chops. It took a couple of months for the
insults and torment to stop. I had to fight to earn respect.

Eventually, I became "boss" at the school. I made a rule that all
younger and older children were to treat one another equally. The
younger children looked up to me, and I gave them the job of reporting the bullies to me. I always confronted the bullies. But my biggest
goal was to preach love and friendship.

December 5 rolled around again. I polished my shoes and set
them up on the windowsill, waiting for Santa Claus. Faithfully, Santa
showed up the following day bearing gifts for all of us. I recited no
Hanukkah prayers this December nor would I ever again. All the students, teachers, and counselors were Christians. Many of them didn't
know a thing about Hanukkah. I expected that I should have felt
some sort of a loss, but didn't. I was no longer a part of the Jewish
faith. I felt a sense of obligation and thankfulness to the school for
providing me with food, shelter, education, and support.

During Christmastime, most of the children went home. Those
who remained, such as myself, were labeled "poor." The staff members knew I was without a family, and they allowed me to eat with
them. I was also free to do as I pleased, and I usually roamed the city.

January was an exciting month, filled with eventful competition.
A gymnastics tournament was to take place at the end of January. It
was being held for the local deaf and hearing schools. My gymnastic
skills were improving, but I wasn't good enough yet to participate in
the competition. Instead, I opted to work on my skills for the local

deaf and hearing school chess tournament, which would also take place in January. Our gymnastics team lost to the hearing teams who were simply better. We lost the chess tournament, too, placing at the midpoint among the teams. But I won all my matches.

The dull, gray days of winter took over after those competitions, and the regular routines of school life marked the days until Holy Week. It was Good Friday, the transition from Lent to Eastertime, and the end of a school day. I noticed my friend, Károly Radonics, with red marks all over his face and asked him what had happened. He explained that he had just finished lunch, and he and his friends decided to go up to the third floor to grab their homework books. The priest's room was located next door to the class where their homework books were located. Deciding to be nosy, he peeked through the keyhole to the priest's room and witnessed the priest eating salami. Károly knew that nobody was allowed to eat meat on Good Friday and urged his friends to witness the priest's behavior. Each friend took a turn looking through the keyhole. Then, they all went back downstairs, not saying a word about it. During the next Bible study session, Károly confronted the priest, telling him that he saw him eat the salami on Good Friday. The priest angrily walked over to Károly and, in front of the other students, belted Károly across the face. I felt so sorry for him. I recalled my time in the ghetto yet again, remembering the religious hypocrites I had encountered.

In the middle of spring, Pál called me into his office. He encouraged me to go to college. My academic skills had impressed him. Knowing that graduation was just months away, he wanted to ensure my future. He suggested that I become an engineer, explaining that the government program would provide food, clothes, and a dorm if I decided to pursue that field. I agreed, although I wondered whether it was too good to be true.

Together, we applied for a scholarship. I also asked Pál about acquiring other money as a means of support. I no longer had allowance or tip money. He was unable to help me out and didn't know of anyone else who could. For several weeks, I worried. I was sure I had no chance of being accepted to college, and I didn't want to face rejection. So, I decided not to pursue the college route. I told Pál my decision, and he was extremely disappointed.

The next evening, feeling that a huge weight had been lifted off my shoulders, a group of us went up to the mountains to gaze at the moon and solar system through huge telescopic lenses at an observatory station. It was fascinating. After gazing into space, we headed back down the mountain. I spotted two men playing chess. I could see that one of the men was about to make a bad move. I approached him and pointed out his error, lingering to watch the rest of the game. When they were done, the man invited me to play. We played and talked about work throughout the game. As soon as I won the game, he suggested that I play his friend. I beat his friend, too. The man was impressed and invited me to join the hearing chess team. He also offered me a job as a mechanic, repairing the monstrous telescopes. I told him that I had to decline his offer to become a member of his chess team because I was already on the deaf chess team and felt obligated to them. But, I told him, I was interested in the mechanic job. The man wanted me to commit to both or forget the offer altogether. I turned it down.

In June 1950, I proceeded with my graduation ceremonies. The event was both a major accomplishment and a loss. All the children who graduated went home to find jobs or go to college. I had no place to stay, and I had no job. I felt a sense of numbness as I recognized that I was still fighting for stability in my life. However, after my encounter with the hearing chess player, I knew I could somehow find a job. I realized how important it was for me to branch out and communicate with other people.

Dr. Kanizsai had been keeping tabs on me. He contacted me and suggested that I live at the institute. However, he stated a condition that I had to actively seek out employment. I was interested in mechanical work, but all the jobs listed required that I have a mechanical background. I found an apprenticeship, a machinist position that offered schooling and hands-on experience. I applied and was immediately accepted. All I had to do was undergo a complete medical exam. During the medical exam, the doctor filled out the form and told me to return it to the company to which I had applied. I didn't know it at the time, but the doctor had indicated on the form that I would be unable to work on any machinery because of my deafness. I took the form back to the company. The manager of the company read the note from the doctor and laughed, saying, "That doctor is crazy." He twirled his index finger around the temple of his head, showing me the sign for crazy. He told me what the doctor's note said and explained that the company had deaf employees who were capable of doing all machine work. The manager crunched up the doctor's report in his hands, tossed it in the trash, and said, "You're hired."

I was so excited. I immediately went to visit Sári néni. I told her of my good fortune and related what had been going on. She told me how proud she was of me. She handed me a bag of toiletries, telling me that I would need it for my new living quarters.

CHAPTER 13 (1950–1952)

THE MECHANICAL TRADE SCHOOL

THE APPRENTICESHIP that I had been accepted to included a three-year program at a mechanical trade school called the United Izzo Tungsram Electric, Inc. The company was controlled by both American and western European firms. Because the Hungarian government did not have the rights to the wolfram (tungsten), they couldn't control the firm. The wolfram consisted of a hard, brittle, metallic element used in materials and electrical elements that had to tolerate high temperatures. Its most common use was in lamp filaments. The Hungarian government needed the company's business and, therefore, did not impose its communistic laws on the school.

The school provided boarding; however, no rooms were available at the time of enrollment. Dr. Kanizsai allowed me to stay on at the institute because I had satisfied him by landing a job. I had to commute between the school and the institute. After two months, the trade school finally had a bed available. I transferred permanently to the school, making it my new home. The school provided me with meals and a bit of pocket change.

Approximately five hundred students, all of whom were boys, lived in the one large dorm building. Each room contained five bunk beds and housed ten students. The counselor of the dorm assigned each bed.

The school taught primarily hearing students, although approximately fifteen deaf students attended. Two of the deaf students stayed in my dorm, and two were at my level. Our schooling, which included chemistry, design, mechanics, and so forth, took place three days a week. For the other three days, we performed general machine work, which included plumbing, lathe work, and blacksmith-type work.

The school had a very strict, military-like atmosphere. Students were required to wear uniforms and to keep them cleaned and pressed.

I had only one uniform and, therefore, washed it nightly. I didn't have an iron, so I placed my uniform between the mattresses at night to keep it neat and pressed.

Everyone was required to wake up at five o'clock each morning, get dressed, and march outside to the field for exercises. If we did not exercise, we couldn't receive a meal ticket. Without a meal ticket, we couldn't receive breakfast, and no lunch was packed for us to eat while at school or work. Unless we had a bad storm, we had to exercise in all weather, even snow. I never missed a day of exercise because I knew what it was like to go hungry.

Another strict regulation was evening inspection. A counselor scrutinized each room, checking to see that we met certain standards, including having clean feet. At about ten o'clock every evening, while we were sleeping, the counselor lifted the sheets, inspecting our feet. If anyone was caught with dirty feet, he was woken up and told to go wash his feet. The student was given half an hour to clean up. Usually, the counselor would come back later and do another inspection, giving special attention to those who had had dirty feet. Any student who still hadn't cleaned up properly was dowsed with a bucket of water. His mattress would end up getting soaking wet and would remain wet for a long time, which provided a strong reminder to maintain clean feet. Thank goodness it never happened to me.

I had plenty of friends at my new school. Most of the students liked me because I was a competent table tennis player. I also became more involved with the deaf club, attending on a daily basis and involving myself with as many deaf functions as possible. I became good friends with a guy named Herman who was the youth junior champion for chess in Budapest. His accomplishments motivated me to improve my chess skills.

Although I had plenty of new friends, I missed my close friends from the institute. Ábrahám was now a part of my past. Ernö had left to live in Israel. Márkus had moved to New York. In addition, I had not received any letters from anyone in my family for a while. Everyone had moved to new locations, including myself. I felt lonely; I was deaf, feeling isolated in a hearing world.

Not until summertime would I get a letter. Dr. Kanizsai contacted me, saying that a letter had arrived for me at the institute. It was from Sándor. I was relieved that someone had made contact with me, although I did wonder why the rest of my siblings had not stayed in touch. I wrote back, asking him for everyone's address.

Up until now, I had not been doubtful about communism, but I began to seriously question the glory it had received. The Labor Party had grown quite powerful. Everything was now government-controlled, even the farms. No one was permitted to own a factory or business. As a result of the governmental power, many people from the farms and businesses were out of work. These people were forced to leave their homes and search for work in Budapest. People had become dissatisfied with their lives. I was disgusted at the way people had lost their rights to the government.

At the same time, the Americans were supporting the Greeks in their quest for capitalism. Those who favored communism in Greece ended up fleeing to Budapest or to other communist countries. The

Here I am, at the far right, in my apprentice uniform, with my table tennis team. From left to right, Tamás, György, Jenő, Pál, and me.

problem was that the Hungarian government was providing jobs to these Greeks before taking care of the Hungarian people.

Eventually, people began complaining about communism. Anyone who got caught complaining was arrested by secret police and sent to jail. It became a common occurrence that family members would search for their loved ones in jail only to find that they weren't there. They would be dismayed to learn that anti-Communists were being sent to Siberia. Naturally, I became very careful about participating in any discussions that did not support communism. I had learned it was best to say nothing.

In my second year of school, my counselor and I met to discuss future job possibilities. He was concerned that my name would create an obstacle in finding a job because it obviously identified me as a Jew. He recommended that I change my name. I was willing to make this change because I knew a different name would shield me from the anti-Semitic attitudes. The law stated that only a godparent could change a person's first name if the parents were dead. But because everyone was dead, I had to pick another first name that started with the letter *I*. Strangely enough, I felt a bit resentful toward my father for giving me such an identifiable Jewish name. I decided my first name would now be Imre. My last name also had to start with the letter of my original last name, which was *D*. The counselor suggested that I select Diossy, Daranyi, or Dunai. I picked the third choice. I was to become Imre Dunai.

To have my name changed, I sent a request letter to the city clerk. I received a quick response, stating that they had accepted Dunai as my last name but not Imré as my first name. The clerk needed documentation showing that my parents or godparents had given me the name of Imre. I had to go in person to the city clerk's office and explain that I had lost my parents and godparents in the war and had no proof. The clerk found my original birth certificate on file but found no record that my parents and godparents had perished. Luckily, he still granted me the name change. Unfortunately, the name change required a nominal fee. I pleaded with the clerk that, because of my orphan status, I had no money. He generously waived the fee, hoping that the welfare assistance would cover my costs. I was now Imre Dunai.

At work, I continued to perform beyond the school's expectations. Inside, however, I struggled with conflicting feelings. I felt that my performance was better than most of the other students. I felt dissatisfied with the pocket change I was earning. I felt uneasy and wanted to move forward at a quicker pace, and yet, many times, I felt like giving up.

During break times, I lingered in the cafeteria. On one particular day, another deaf student and I were conversing in sign language. I noticed a hearing student making fun of our communication. The hearing student and I were at the same academic level. I got up from my chair and went over to him. Grabbing a glass of water that was on the table, I tossed it at his face, telling him to back off. The hearing boy grabbed a bottle of water and attempted to throw it at me. I quickly put my hand out, and the water spilled all over him. The hearing boy and two of his hearing friends began to beat me up. Quickly, several student bystanders pulled the three boys off of me because fighting was not permitted in the factory. Anyone who got caught fighting would be terminated.

The foreman heard the ruckus and ordered all of us to his office. I explained why I reacted the way I did and added that I had not physically touched the boy. But, I told him, all three of the boys had attacked me. The three boys were fired. I was lucky. The foreman loved deaf people and believed my story. He said it was a good thing that I hadn't hit back.

At times, I didn't want to go to class. I guess I wanted to rebel. At other times, Károly and I played pranks on the teachers or other students. Károly lived in the city of Budapest and attended the school. One day, we both decided to ditch class because of a good sporting event that was to be held at the deaf club. However, we knew that if we didn't show up to class, we would be punished. To avoid punishment, we came up with a plan to have our classes canceled in time for the event. We unscrewed the two light bulbs in the classroom and placed small pieces of paper between the sockets and the contacts on

Students from the trade school. Károly is on the far right of the second row. I'm behind him in the third row, second from the right.

the bulbs. The school day usually continued past nightfall, and the lights would need to be switched on to continue the class.

Dusk came, and our teacher went to flip on the light switch—no lights. Károly and I looked at each other. We were ecstatic, knowing our remaining classes would be canceled. Instead, the teacher told us to stay in our seats while he called the janitor to check on the problem. The janitor checked the switch and fuses. He couldn't figure out the problem. To our dismay, classes were not canceled, and instead, the class had to move into the freezing cold gymnasium to finish up our coursework.

The next day, an electrician was called in to locate the problem. He knocked out a large section of the wall to check the wiring. Károly and I were walking down the hallway and saw the electrician performing his work. In a panic, we dashed down the hallway and into the classroom, quickly unscrewing the light bulbs and removing the paper. The students in our class knew what we had done, but they kept quiet. The teacher came in and flipped on the light switch. To his amazement, the lights came on. He said nothing at that point, although he had his suspicions of foul play.

The next day, the teacher questioned the hearing students who attended classes in the morning hours. They denied knowing about the problem. It was then the deaf students' turn for questioning. During our interrogation, one student almost spilled the story but remained silent after getting a pinch from Károly. We never got caught.

Toward the end of the school year, I realized that I didn't want to attend another year of school. Perhaps I was beginning to outgrow the pranks and the rebellion. I had known for a while that I was as competent as and probably equal to the professionals who were employed by the firm, and I wanted to use my skills. I requested the opportunity to take my mechanical test early. The school granted my request.

The test site was at another location. The proctor tested my abilities by giving me different types of piecework to be performed on a variety of machines. The test lasted from eight in the morning until two in the afternoon. When the test ended, the proctor looked at me and said, "Pass," yet I was unsure whether his pronouncement meant that I could actually graduate.

Back at my work site, I waited apprehensively for my instructor, Vida Gabor's reaction. Although I felt confident, I worried about jinxing myself. Finally, Vida appeared and began applauding me. He showed me the comment on the report from the testing site, which said, "Imre is a gifted boy." I could see that Vida was deeply pleased that I had passed the exam.

The school and the firm were equally proud that I had passed, both boasting that they had trained me well. The school had a graduation ceremony for its fifteen hundred students. Nine students were presented with awards. I was one of them. In addition, the firm offered me a permanent position with better pay, working in a different department.

CHAPTER 14 (1952–1956)

THE DEAF CLUB AND
THE COMFORTS OF HOME

I WILLINGLY accepted the job at the electric company. However, because I was now an employee and not a student, I could no longer live at the school. I was a little disappointed that I had to find my own place. Apartments were hard to come by and were very expensive. At the same time, I was fed up with living in a military atmosphere with a group of people sharing a room.

The first place I moved into had terrible conditions. The woman landlord was bossy and manipulative, and tried to control everyone's lives. Every room housed two people. My living arrangements provided no more than a place to sleep.

In hopes of finding a homelike atmosphere, I continuously searched for a better apartment, making many moves. Luckily, my involvement at the deaf club allowed me breathing space outside the room rentals. In essence, the deaf club was really my home and a major part of my life where I would participate in sports and daily social activities. It was the positive aspect of my existence.

In our competition with the hearing team of Budapest, the deaf club's chess team made a historical mark that excited us all. I was player number six, representing the ten-member deaf chess team. Player number one was the strongest player, and player number ten, the weakest. The hearing team sat facing our lineup of strength at a long buffet-style table. We won five-and-a-half games, and the hearing team won four-and-a-half games. For the first time in the history of the deaf chess team of Budapest, we had won first place.

I had been visiting Sári néni quite regularly after work. I knew she wanted to move to England, and every time I visited her, she shared her disappointment of being rejected by the Hungarian Communist government. Now, her dream had come true. Her third request had

For the first time in history, the deaf club's chess team, on the left, triumphed over the hearing team, on the right.

been successful, and her application for immigration status had been approved. As we said our good-byes and hugged, we promised to find each other in the future, unsure whether we'd ever see each other again. She also promised to write to me with her new home address. I knew I would miss her very much. She and her family had been my second family. Now, I was alone, away from the people who were dear to my heart.

I felt like parts of my life were crumbling again. Apartment living was awkward. Sári néni left for England. And I was no longer happy working for the firm. They had me on a schedule of rotating shifts, which was very hard to get used to, and the pay was unfair. The pay was based on a system of completing piecework, with the foreman being responsible for disseminating the work. The foreman consistently gave me the lower paying piecework while distributing the higher paying pieces to his buddies. I never complained to him, because I felt too new on the job to object.

By 1953, I decided I had to quit the firm and find other employment. At the deaf club, I shared my frustrations about work with my friend, Kálmán Kentner. He told me not to worry about getting a job.

His employer was the City Gas Company, and he promised to inquire about job opportunities for me.

The next day, I saw Kálmán at the club. He gave me information on the few positions available at his work site. I was so pleased by his thoughtfulness. The following day after work, I went to the City Gas Company and applied for a position. About a week later, I was hired. My employment with the gas company would end up continuing until 1957 and would be the stepping-stone for my future. I went straight to the electric company after receiving the news and gave my notice. They were flabbergasted that I was quitting and told me that I'd have a difficult time finding a job. It felt good to tell them I already had one.

At the gas company, I started out as an apprentice. I guess my title was gas pipe fitter or general machinist. The job was interesting. I had to look at blueprints and existing parts and then make new ones. Everything was new to me. I had to use my brain. Working on the machines gave me great satisfaction and pride. And the factory chief gave me a lot of respect.

The chess team of the Budapest Deaf Club.

Kálmán Kentner, a friend from the deaf club, helped me get a job as a general machinist at the City Gas Company.

As a machinist, I used calipers, micrometers, gauges, and various measuring tools for threads, bits, oil, and so on. I had to make parts to put in the gas meter so the gas meter could be read. If the parts in the gas meter wore out, I replaced them. If we didn't have a part, I manufactured it.

The work seemed to come to me naturally. I just had to concentrate on whatever I was ordered to do and do it. The company required me to complete a quota of parts on a daily basis. Quotas were based on productivity. For example, I could make twelve parts in three or four hours compared to other machinists who took an entire day. I tried not to work too fast; otherwise, the managers would have given me more and more to do. I tried to maintain a balance. Whatever they ordered, I made sure I provided it on time, which they loved.

At my last apartment rental, the landlord, a deaf Jewish widow named Mrs. Rosenfeldne, set me up in a room with one woman and another man. It was an acceptable arrangement, and I liked the widow and her son. Every Saturday when Mrs. Rosenfeldne's son visited, I was invited for lunch. In no time, he and I became friends.

At the gas company, I began as an apprentice and quickly learned the job, impressing my managers.

His name was originally Rosenfeld, but he changed it to Lajos Révész. We always discussed politics. He had become a big Communist Party member after his experience in a hard-labor camp. He shared with me his views on communism and his reactions to capitalism, including the experience that had made him anticapitalistic. While in the hard-labor camp, he had written a letter to his very wealthy uncle asking him for financial help. His uncle responded, "Here is the money, and don't ask me for any more." He couldn't believe that his own flesh-and-blood uncle could use such harsh words. From that point on, he hated rich people and all capitalists.

Lajos was sensitive to deaf people, deaf news, and deaf culture. He kept abreast by reading a deaf newspaper, which sometimes gave the impression to others that he was deaf himself. In fact, one day as he was reading his newspaper for the deaf on a park bench, a couple of hearing men began making fun of him, calling him deaf and dumb. They did not know that Lajos was hearing. Lajos became angry and hurt at how the men were mocking someone they thought was deaf. He saw a policeman and casually went to speak to the officer. He explained the story and told the policeman to arrest the two men. Lajos had power in the Communist Party, and the policeman knew it. He arrested the two men then and there.

My friendship with Kálmán was growing closer and was becoming an asset. Aside from working together at the City Gas Company, a job that he had helped me find, we spent a lot of time together at the deaf club, playing chess and table tennis. After awhile, Kálmán introduced me to his family. Kálmán's parents were also deaf and practicing Catholics. His deaf brother was named Sándor like my own brother, and his hearing sister was named Vilma. They enjoyed my company and invited me to dinner on a regular basis. Kálmán's parents grew to like me very much. After several months of visiting, they insisted that I move in with them.

I gladly accepted their offer, paying them rent. In return, I had a wonderful home. Mother Kentner provided me with my own bedroom. She kept my room clean, changed the bedding, laundered my clothes, and made my meals. The Kentners made me an integral part of their family. We shared all the holidays such as Christmas and Easter together.

Father Kentner, or Antal, was an avid Bible reader, always expressing his views and sharing Bible stories with me. He also spoke against Russia. I never criticized him, nor did I tell him I did not believe in God. However, he did open my mind to possibilities of truths in the Bible that I had doubted before. I was still skeptical of any belief system.

Kálmán and I dreamed of seeing the world. I fantasized about traveling. Naturally, I longed to visit my childhood home where Salgo and Lenke were residing. But dreams were not enough. I wanted to travel for real and decided to start the process rolling. I made up my mind that visiting my birthplace would be the first adventure. The first roadblock was to get a letter to Salgo. My home was no longer named Magyar Komjat. It was now called Velky Komjata, Russia, under communist rule, or Komjata for short.

Luckily, in my last room rental, I had met Lajos, who had been in a hard-labor camp and, later, had fled to Russia, becoming fluent in Russian. I decided to pay him a visit and ask for his assistance so I could correspond with Lenke and Salgo. He was more than willing to assist me in translating Salgo's address from Hungarian to Russian. I sent a letter the very next day. Within a few weeks, I received a letter from Salgo. He was anxious for me to visit, which made my dreams grow all the more real. Now, I had to find a way to get permission to leave the country.

I began to feel more secure in my daily life, but I still struggled with larger social, environmental, and political issues. Although I

Kálmán took this photo of me with Szidi Koszta, on the left, and his girlfriend, Kato Öz, on the right.

The Kentners opened their home to me and I quickly came to feel like part of the family. This is a self-portrait I took while staying in their house.

was no longer overboard pro-Communist, I joined the Deaf Communist Seminary in 1952, and would stay active until 1955. In this seminary, deaf adults taught me the politics of communism, comparing it to imperialism, socialism, capitalism, and facism, which allowed me to understand the behavior of each group. I joined to plan for the future. I was hoping that my membership would allow me to eventually visit my home and part of my family because I figured I would eventually need to apply for a passport. I attended the seminary on a weekly basis, knowing I had to play the game of life—a game of fate and survival.

Sometime in 1954, I visited Vilma's place. She had been suffering from a persistent cough and had just been diagnosed with tuberculosis. She needed medication, but no penicillin was available in Budapest. After a week or so of futile searching for the penicillin, her condition grew worse. I offered to write a letter to Irén, requesting that she get the medicine for Vilma. About three weeks later, Vilma received the penicillin from Irén. It took several weeks for Vilma to begin responding to the medication. I will never forget how thankful she was of Irén and me.

By 1955, I was a leader in table tennis. A big international tournament was coming up. Our team was second place in Budapest and had never made it to the play-offs. But this year, we had an outstanding team. We were set to play against the Romanian team. I was to play against a man without hands. At first, I was mesmerized as he held the paddle tightly between his crossed wrists. Consequently, he won the first match; then I found his weak spot. I beat him two matches to one. Our team ultimately beat the Romanian team, a conquest that was a feather in our cap. After the tournament, our team celebrated wildly at the deaf club. Nominations were made for new members of the board, and I was elected treasurer.

My job and home life were stable, so I decided to prepare to visit my birthplace. Fortunately, I had made an acquaintance with a Hungarian Communist named Mr. Kékési, who was a secret service government agent working for the passport department. Mr. Kékési also happened to have deaf parents and was willing to help me. He knew that I was attending the Communist Seminary and, therefore, was comfortable in assisting me. He told me that obtaining a passport wasn't easy and involved certain steps. First, I would need letters of support, which I received from the Communist Seminary and the City Gas Company. The second thing I needed was a recent photo of myself. The last item was identification: I needed something that listed my birthplace with my name. I was extremely glad that my previous counselor had wisely advised me to change my name. My former name of Izráel most likely would have damaged my chances for obtaining the passport, which I received shortly after submitting all the documentation.

In the meantime, I received a letter from Sándor. He had moved to Israel and was now working on a cargo ship. He took the ship job so he could travel and see the world. He sent me a package of clothes, a full three-piece suit, and a twenty-four-dollar gift certificate for the department store, IKKA. The certificate was particularly useful because I was not able to use foreign currency. Instead of sending money, Sándor had been sending me a certificate for twenty-four dollars every two weeks for about one year. I used the certificates to buy clothing, shoes, and wool fabric, which I took to have specially made suits, sports jackets, and a full-length winter coat because the winters were freezing.

The tailor who made my clothes was a Jewish deaf man named Sam Fuch. He was a Holocaust survivor, like me. Sam's stories of his past were interesting, especially his accounts of getting a job as a tailor during the massive unemployment of 1940 and his secret work for Prime Minister Nagy. Searching for a job in 1940, Sam and nine hearing applicants competed for a position at a department store by each making a suit to demonstrate his tailoring skills. When each applicant completed his suit, he had to leave it with his name on a piece of paper in the pocket of the suit jacket. A committee then inspected the suits to determine which was best tailored. Of course, Sam's suit was selected, and the committee members were amazed that he was deaf. But his lack of understandable speech did not stand in his way. They recognized his talent and quickly hired him as a tailor. Later, in 1946 or 1947, the Hungarian Prime Minister, Ferenc Nagy, went to see Sam privately at Sam's apartment. Nagy told him that he needed several suits made because he had lost in the election and was planning to leave for western Europe. Nagy knew that, if Russia occupied Hungary, he and Hungary would be merely puppets of the communist government. Sam made his suits.

CHAPTER 15 (1956)

A VISIT HOME TO KOMJATA

MY PASSPORT finally arrived. I had to go to the Soviet Embassy and show them my passport, my point of destination, and my planned length of stay. With that information, I got the visa stamp. I couldn't stop looking at it. I was getting nervous about seeing my homeland.

The passport couldn't have come at a better time because the gas company had given me a three-week paid vacation. I sent a letter to Salgo, letting him know my itinerary. Salgo responded, saying that both he and Lenke would be expecting me. I was so excited. I constantly thought about going back. I wanted to see my home—the place where I was born. I was homesick.

I arrived at 8:00 A.M. at the Russian border in the city of Chop (formerly known as Csap). A Russian border patrol asked me for my passport. He must have realized I couldn't understand him. Luckily, he knew how to speak Hungarian. He asked me the reason for my visit. I told him that I'd come to see my homeland and visit my brother and sister. He accepted my answer and let me pass. Salgo was there to greet me—a surprise for me. I had not expected him to be waiting. We hugged, and we cried.

Together, we got on the bus going north to the city of Ungvar (now known as Uzhgorod) to notify the police department that I had arrived in town. It was standard procedure for all visitors. The police stamped my passport. We then boarded the bus heading for Komjata via Munkács (now known as Munkacsevo). Along the way, Salgo told me that Lenke was unable to meet me at the train depot because she was busy at home taking care of her daughters. It had been a long time since Lenke and I had last seen each other.

When the bus stopped, we had to walk with my suitcase along the highway and pathways for nearly a mile. The farmers all looked out their windows as we passed, trying to figure out who I was. At about three in the afternoon, we arrived at home. The place felt empty, spiritless. All of the personal effects were gone. I mean everything—furniture, photographs, memorabilia, jewelry, books—everything! Although Salgo lived in our home, it wasn't the same. I felt an aching sensation down to my bones, a simultaneous sense of pain and loss. Suddenly overcome by grief, I sneaked off to Irén and Magda's old bedroom and cried hard, agonizing over the loss of my family. I recited the memories of the things in life I once had and what had happened to my family. I wanted to share my emotions with Salgo, but I couldn't bring myself to do it. I didn't know how. I also felt uneasy having just been introduced to Salgo's family. His wife Ruth was sweet, and they had a beautifully shy daughter named Gabriella. Ruth's first born had died. Now, she was pregnant with her third child. I finally regained my composure and joined them.

We stayed up very late the first night. Salgo told me about the farm police and the sheriff with the black hat sporting a rooster feather who had rounded up the Jewish settlers while receiving assistance from some of the farmers who had yelled, "There's a Jew! That's a Jew!" Christian neighbors had helped with the extraction of Jews from their homes, too. The Arrow Cross militants had posted a schedule and had deported the settlers, filling the trains to capacity. Those deported usually trekked an average of four miles to reach the death train.

During the first couple of days, Salgo and I played a lot of chess. He couldn't believe how well I could play. I kept winning the games. So Salgo decided to invite the county's best chess player to play against me. Unfortunately, I lost to him. That didn't stop Salgo. The next day, he took me to the local bar. Everybody seemed to remember me, saying hello and shaking my hand. They told me they thought I was dead—not because I was a Jew but because I was deaf and had been very young. I couldn't believe they remembered me; it had been twelve years. I was a child then. All the same, Salgo and I beat them at chess.

I didn't know it at the time, but Salgo had placed bets on me. All the chess players had laughed, knowing they could beat a deaf chess player. But, the joke was on them because Salgo filled his pockets with money while I declared myself the winner.

A few more days went by, and I went to visit Lenke. I was a little bit nervous to see her, but when we saw each other, we hugged and we both cried. She cried the most, begging me for forgiveness for causing my deafness. Once again, I didn't know what to say or how to react. Yet, I told her to please not worry; I was a grown man. I tried to comfort her, telling her that it had been an accident and not her fault—and that I was happy to see her.

Lenke had a nice husband named Bela and two beautiful daughters. Helena was four years old and Marilyn was two. Helena, who was very smart for her age, came up to me constantly, challenging me to speak to her. She spoke a little Hungarian. Bela was originally from a village called Nagyszollos, located approximately thirteen kilometers from our town of Komjata. Nagyszollos meant "grand" or "big grapes." However, with the changing of the borders, the town of Nagyszollos had become the town of Vinogradov, which also had the same meaning. The front of their home was a bar, and Bela made the best hot wine. All the local military officers, retirees, police, and others came regularly after their shifts to drink at the bar. They were all very nice people.

During my two-day stay with Lenke, she encouraged me to hurry up and get married. However, she told me I should marry a hearing girl, not a deaf girl. She was afraid that if I had children with a deaf woman, I'd end up with deaf children. I disagreed with her, telling her that if I married a hearing woman, the two of us would have difficulty communicating. I also told her that I was comfortable being deaf and enjoyed all my deaf friends. It took a while, but eventually, she realized the point I was trying to make.

Back in Salgo's house, I reveled in Ruth's cooking. One morning for breakfast, she cooked me goose liver. It had been almost twelve years since I had eaten any, and it was the best I'd ever tasted. I asked her why it was so good. She said that her secret was in the feed. She hand-fed her geese an abundance of fresh corn seed, not ground corn, until the geese were nice and plump. Goose liver wasn't the only great meal, however. Ruth was a fine cook through and through.

I also had the opportunity to visit the Ungvar Deaf Association. When I arrived, they were holding a meeting. A man approached me, asking me where I was from. I told the man that I was from Budapest but originally from Komjata. I could tell that the man recognized me by the look in his eyes. He introduced himself as the postman's son

My sister Lenke in 1950 in front of our farmhouse in Russia.

from Komjata. Now, I made a connection to my past, recalling why the postman was so nice to me years ago. It was because his son was deaf. One more of the puzzle pieces of my life fell into place. Unfortunately, the meeting at the Ungvar Deaf Association was foreign to me because the language used was Russian. I decided to stay anyway and tried hard to decipher the meeting, relying on body language. The postman's son tried to interpret, too.

During my stay in Komjata, I walked around the village, observing the changes. What had once been two Jewish synagogues in the village were now milk factories. Only nineteen Jewish families remained. I also took special notice that the clothing and scarves that the women wore were of poor quality and decided that, when I returned to Budapest, I would buy plenty of fabric and scarves to sell to the townspeople during my next visit.

The trip home to Komjata had been the worst of my experiences since the war. The pain was intense, nearly unbearable. Yet, I left Russia feeling satisfied, with a sense of closure. When I returned to Budapest, everyone at work and at the deaf club asked me about my trip. Naturally, I spoke highly of Russia. I also went to see Mr. Kékési and told him about my journey. I asked him whether it was possible for me to visit Russia again in the fall. He said that it was no problem and that when the time arrived he would issue me another passport without question. He told me he was happy with my high esteem of Russia. I prepared myself for the next trip by purchasing the fabric and scarves in advance.

My job at the gas company was stable but not very challenging. Nevertheless, knowing that I was needed, especially by the foreman, did feel good. I was supposed to be working on the lathe, but another foreman kept pulling me to work on the mill and on other machines. Both foremen kept me busy doing a variety of things. At one point, the chief asked me which foreman I preferred working under. I told him that I preferred to continue building parts but not working for the foreman who was in charge of the lathe. The chief decided to let me stay where I was, which pleased the other foreman. He had been a sergeant in the Hungarian army. He was very strict with all the employees, except for me. With me, he was relaxed and friendly. We had lengthy conversations at break time.

Six months later in September, I was offered another two-week paid vacation from my employer. I decided to take another trip back to Russia. This time, I received my passport without all the red tape. I stayed with Salgo and his family for two weeks. During my stay, Ruth finally had her baby—a son. I also met a nice deaf girl, but I decided not to have an ongoing relationship with her for two reasons. First, we spoke different languages, and second, we lived miles apart. Salgo and I went back to the local bar for a chess rematch. Again, I won all the matches, and Salgo was content with the prize money weighing down his pockets. I was successful in selling the fabric and scarves I had brought from Budapest. The leftovers I was unable to sell I gave away as gifts. With the money I made from selling the fabric and scarves, I bought a good Russian camera called a Zorkij.

As soon as I returned from Russia, I went again to visit Mr. Kékési to thank him for the passport. I told him how appreciative I was and presented him with a gift of cigarettes and cigars. He was very thankful.

I also went to the deaf club to tell my friends about my visit to my homeland. I was surprised when my friend, György Weltner told me of his plans to marry Maria Ivankay. I was surprised that he would wed a Catholic woman. However, György was an intelligent man, and I knew that whatever decision he made was the right choice for him. Although I was surprised, I was not disturbed because I didn't hold all Catholics responsible for the Holocaust. However, György indicated that Maria's parents weren't too pleased that their daughter was marrying a Jew. Out of respect for Maria's parents, György decided to convert to Catholicism. He wanted to please Maria's parents and satisfy Maria by getting married in the Roman Catholic Church. His conversion would make the process possible.

In the meantime, I was eager to learn how to use my camera. I knew Kálmán was knowledgeable, so I asked him to teach me how to make the necessary camera adjustments and even how to develop the film. Luckily, the gas company had its own photo lab, and Kálmán was able to teach me the developing process. Finding the process of

film developing fascinating, I joined a local photo club. This move
was a good one for me because the photo club contained a labora-
tory, which meant I had access to a place where I could develop my
film. I grew camera crazy, using a tripod and even taking self-
portraits with my special built-in timer.

The wedding day had arrived for György and Maria. I was not
invited, but I went to the church out of respect. I brought my camera along and stayed busy taking photographs of everyone. Nobody
paid any real attention to what I was doing. I was very impressed to
see that György's father had shown up at the church. He, too, had
much respect toward his son and toward Maria's family. As a gift, he
gave the couple his condominium and purchased a new home for
himself.

The next day I processed the photos. I couldn't believe how crisp
and clear they turned out. I presented them to György and Maria as a
wedding gift. They were surprised and very thankful because there
had been no one else with a camera at their wedding to record the
event. They had been so wrapped up with excitement that they didn't
realize what I had been doing there.

The following month, I received a letter from the Swedish Embassy in Budapest. Magda had requested a visa be made on my behalf
so I could visit her. I knew Magda was planning to do it sometime in
the future, but I hadn't expected the letter at this time. I was intensely
excited that I could fulfill more of my dream and wanted desperately
to go to Sweden. I shared the news with Kálmán. He wished he could
go but was unable to join me because the ability to go required that
one have familial relations at the destination.

I had to figure out how I would obtain another passport. Naturally, Mr. Kékési came to mind. I decided to see him immediately
and told him of my sister's request to the Swedish Embassy. He
seemed a bit apprehensive about this venture. He told me that this
request would require a board meeting to be held at the Ministry of
Domestic Affairs. The board would have to deliberate and determine
whether or not it would be permissible for me to leave the country.
I was eager, and in my heart, my dreams to venture west to see the

world seemed very possible. I had been to Russia twice now and felt satisfied. I was ready for the next step of my adventure and future.

By the middle of October, the ministry held a hearing for my passport. I had to respond to a series of questions before the board. They wanted to know my intentions for wanting to go to Sweden. I explained that as a result of the war, my family was no longer intact, that I had lived twelve years without family near me, and that I hadn't seen Magda or Irén since 1944. In addition, I pointed out, I still felt a tremendous loss, and seeing other members of my family would help me heal some of my wounds. I expressed my gratitude to the government for previously granting me a passport to visit Salgo and Lenke in Russia. I added that the trip to Russia had helped me to reach a feeling of satisfaction and closure. In closing, I reiterated how long it had been since I had seen Magda or Irén.

After the board listened to my story and plea, they asked me to leave the room while they deliberated. The minutes that passed felt like hours. I felt comforted knowing that Mr. Kékési would put in his positive vote and support on my behalf. He wanted to grant me a passport to visit my sisters in Sweden.

When the deliberations ended, they summoned me back into the boardroom. They agreed, and granted me a three-month passport to Sweden, noting that it would take approximately two weeks to receive. They told me that their decision was based on my excellent record in the Communist Seminary and my involvement in the communist movement. Ironically, they didn't know that I had never become a member of the Communist Party.

I was totally elated and headed straight for the deaf club to share the news with my friends. Most of them laughed at me, saying they felt sorry for me. They also told me that I was a dreamer and was fooling myself. They didn't believe the government would grant me a passport. I ignored them because I trusted Mr. Kékési's word. I also realized that my deaf friends had never taken the steps necessary to plan for their futures as I had done.

While preparing for the trip to Sweden, I realized that I would need a different form of currency. I went to the bank, but they said they could not give me U.S. dollars or any form of western European currency. However, they could make a paperwork transaction to pay for my train ticket out of eastern Germany to Sweden. The banker made it clear that it was forbidden to have U.S. dollars or any western European currency on hand. In my view, it was a ridiculous rule, and I knew I had to think of another way to get money.

I came up with a brilliant and ambitious idea. I knew a man who was deaf and blind named Andor Bauer. Prior to World War II, he had been the secretary for the deaf sports club. During the war, he had been blinded by shards of window glass that shot into his eyes during the bombings. His wife had left him shortly after the blinding incident and had moved in with her wealthy sister in Sweden. Although they were no longer together, they still corresponded. I knew that his wife sent him five U.S. dollars every week.

I went to see Andor and told him of my obstacles. He was more than willing to make the exchange because he had a hard time using the dollars. He had to go underground when he needed money, converting the U.S. dollars into communist currency. Over a six-week period, we exchanged my communist currency for thirty of his U.S. dollars.

CHAPTER 16 (1956)

THE REVOLUTION

THE DATE was October 23, 1956, and one of my girlfriends and I decided to go out to a movie. While we were at the theater, students at Szeged University in Budapest gathered outside to listen to students declaring the unfairness of lack of free speech under the communist government. They were fed up with the Russians pillaging Hungary's precious mineral supply, specifically uranium and aluminum. The Hungarians were receiving no compensation. Since the war, the Hungarians' hatred toward the corrupt Soviets had been growing.

The students marched to Parliament Square with their resolute declarations. But someone had tipped off the authorities that a campus protest was under way. After a short time, an ambulance drove by, filled with secret police, and they opened fire on the students. In the interim, the movie ended, and my girlfriend and I parted ways. I noticed that people in the streets were agitated, but I didn't bother to ask anyone what was happening.

By the next morning, a major riot had developed, which could be seen just outside the Kentner's home. No transportation was available. I walked downtown to ask people what was happening. They explained about the university incident that had happened the night before and that had led to the present rioting. I decided to walk over to the City Gas Company. The office was closed, and the employees were on strike. The employees were huddling in groups, discussing the incident and their futures. My view, which I kept to myself, was that, although I still agreed with the communist philosophy of fairness and equality, I no longer accepted communism under Russian influence. Nevertheless, all I could do was think about Sweden. I began to wonder whether this uproar would become an obstacle to my trip.

123

That evening, I watched as the angry people banded together, tying a rope to a huge bronze statue of Stalin. With all their collective might, they succeeded in pulling the statue to the ground. It broke into large chunky pieces. Then, the people grabbed hammers, chisels, and whatever they could get their hands on to break the bronze chunks into smaller pieces. They didn't want the statue resurrected. Everyone was grabbing up the pieces to save as keepsakes. I stayed out of it, strictly remaining an observer. I wasn't about to ruin my chances of going to Sweden.

For a few days, it seemed as though the Hungarians had won the fight—what became known historically as the Hungarian Revolution. The Russians gave up their tanks. But, the conflict wasn't over. The Russians knew they had to fight back because, if they didn't, they would lose control of the entire Eastern European empire.

On November 3 and 4, the Russian army came back from Romania in droves. They blasted their cannons at the city of Budapest, and the fighting ensued for days. The free radio from Germany told the Hungarian people "to keep fighting until blood drips." The Hungarians believed that the western European countries and America would come to their aid. Homes were looted and burned to the ground. Nobody came to assist the weak Hungarians.

After the Russians claimed their victory, they began installing a new governmental body, and the people of Budapest grew anxious about their future. Tremendous chaos, shooting, and lawlessness raged out of control. The borders opened up because no soldiers were available to man the boundaries. Hungarians packed their essentials, leaving their history behind, and headed for the Austrian border, never looking back. They weren't the only ones; many of the Russian soldiers fled, seeking refuge for a better way of life. On the other side of the borders, the Red Cross assisted those people who wanted to start a new life or paid their way to a new country.

I decided it was in my best interest to wait during this uprising, maintaining good faith with Mr. Kékési. I wanted him to know that I was faithful to my country, plus I didn't want to make him look bad. Up until this point, most of my friends had thought I was crazy for trying to obtain a passport through the legal channels. Many of them fled when the borders were opened, begging me to join them. But I liked to do things the straight and honest way. My friends laughed and hounded me. Those who failed to leave the country while the borders were open had no choice but to flee the country when the borders closed. They escaped under trains and by motorcycle through the countryside. The uprising did not begin to calm down until December. I waited anxiously for my passport.

CHAPTER 17 (1957)

FAREWELL TO BUDAPEST

SHORTLY AFTER the New Year, I received my passport. Again, my excitement was the same as when I had received my first passport to visit Komjata. However, this time, I decided not to share my excitement with anyone at the deaf club—only with a few chosen friends and the Kentners.

Kálmán wouldn't be able to say good-bye to me because he was very involved with soccer at the time and was a star at the sport. He had to go to Bulgaria and Romania for competition. He was satisfied with his life even though he was limited to ventures only within Eastern Europe. For him to leave Eastern Europe, he had to have proof of family ties elsewhere.

I immediately went to the Swedish Embassy for the visa stamp. On the same day, I bought a ticket with an itinerary to go to Borås, Sweden, departing January 23. I went home and wrote a letter to Magda, telling her I'd send a telegram to her from Berlin, Germany. Then, I went to the bank to obtain some Czechoslovákian currency and German deutsch marks for my arrival in Germany. I even made another attempt to obtain western European or Swedish currency but was denied. I was now totally prepared to leave Budapest.

A couple nights later, György and Maria Weltner gave me a secret farewell party. Many deaf Hungarians were present, many of whom would have been against my leaving. Only a handful of my friends knew the real purpose for the party—the others thought it was just a social event.

On January 23, I was ready to say farewell to Budapest. I bought five pounds of winter apples to give to Magda and her husband Meir. The Kentner family accompanied me to the train station, along with the handful of cognizant friends who had attended my farewell party. On the way to the station, the Kentners told me they would miss me but were not sad that I was leaving. Rather, they wished me luck for my future and toward my new life in a new land. Although, I wasn't sure whether I'd stay in Sweden, they had the feeling I would. I promised the Kentners I would stay in touch.

At the train station, everybody advised me not to come back. I hugged and kissed them all, not knowing when I would see them again. I boarded the train that afternoon with only two suitcases, leaving behind most of my clothing and supplies. I didn't want to draw any attention to myself by looking suspicious.

During the evening, the train traveled through Czechoslovákia. It was freezing cold, and I couldn't help but fall in and out of sleep. The train had no heat whatsoever. I dreamed about the ghetto, waking up feeling relieved that I was free. At the Czechoslovákian border, I remained on the train while the engine car changed—a change that brought relief because the new engine had the capacity to heat the other cars. I remained awake until the train arrived in Prague.

My plan had been to stay in Prague for a few days. However, when I exited the train, I was amazed at how freezing cold it was—minus fifteen degrees Celsius. I decided to put my luggage in a holding locker while I checked out the city rather than drag my suitcases with me. I wasn't so sure I wanted to stay.

That afternoon, after enduring frigid temperatures, I retrieved my luggage and decided to reboard the train en route to East Berlin, Germany. The train ride was very warm and comfortable, which allowed me to take a nap. I focused my thoughts on the future rather than on the past. Not knowing the Czechoslovákian or German languages, I kept to myself.

The train arrived late in the evening in East Berlin. I decided to send a telegram to Magda, notifying her of my estimated time of arrival. I found a post office but was having difficulty figuring out how to send the telegram. A German man approached me and offered his assistance. He told me what to do, then took me over to pay for the telegram with my deutsch marks. I was thankful for his explanation and assistance. Believing he was familiar with the area, I decided to ask him whether he could recommend a hotel. He shook his head no and suggested I stay in his home. I hesitated, but he insisted. So I accepted. The kind man fed me dinner and together we drank wine and had awkward conversation. He also provided me with my own clean and tidy room. I was sure it was better than any room rental or hotel I would ever experience.

Early the next morning, the man tried to wake me up. Apparently, he did so by hollering at me through the door. After awhile, he must have grown concerned and entered the room. I awoke to him tapping me on the shoulder. He then motioned to me asking whether I could hear. I indicated no. The man was shocked that we had communicated at all. I, too, was surprised that he had assumed the reason for our difficulty in communication was because of our language difference. We both had used body language. After our equal surprise, we had breakfast together. I washed up, and he accompanied me back to the train station where I thanked him for his generosity.

While waiting at the train station, I saw a vendor selling vodka. I had a few deutsch marks left over and decided to purchase a bottle for the train ride. I was now on my way again. From East Berlin, the train proceeded on land to Sassnitz and to Rostock, Germany. I drank the entire bottle of vodka on the train and got a little drunk. The train then boarded the railway ferry at about noon. We had to wait a couple of hours before departing for Trelleborg, Sweden.

The railway ferry was a Swedish ferry, which would cross the Baltic Sea. On the ferry were actual train tracks onto which the train was loaded. We were then allowed to get off the train, and hurried inside the ferry because of the frigid weather. The interior of the ferry contained a restaurant, a bar, and a duty-free store. Finally, we began moving across the water. It was exhilarating. For the first time in my life, I experienced the sight, aroma, and motion of the sea. On board, I found an abundance of bananas, oranges, figs, salmon, and crab. My experience had been limited to the oranges and figs that Sándor had sent me in a package from Italy. Budapest, being in a communist country, was not open to a variety of fruits for trade. I wanted to purchase some of these incredibly unbelievable foods but was unable to use my eastern European currency and couldn't trade for the Swedish krona. However, a passenger suggested that if I possessed U.S. dollars, I could trade them for the krona. Luckily, I had bought the dollars from Andor at the deaf club before leaving Budapest. I found a passenger who was willing to make the trade and purchased what my heart and taste buds desired.

The ferry ride to Trelleborg was about a four-hour journey. Another engine car hooked up to our train to continue on dry land toward Malmö, Sweden. I was getting excited knowing that I would soon see Magda.

When I arrived at the station, Magda was nowhere to be found. Then, I noticed a Red Cross woman holding up a sign that read, "Imre Dunai." I waved at her, my hands held high. She came forward, and I indicated to her that I was the person named on her sign. She smiled. I reached over, held her hand, and gently gave it a kiss. Her smile widened with a surprised look, and her cheeks turned rosy red. She explained that Magda couldn't leave home to meet me. Meir was sick and she had to take care of her baby. We would spend the night in a hotel, she added, and board another train that would ultimately take us to the town where Magda lived.

The next morning, the Red Cross woman took me to the barbershop. She suggested that a good shave would give me a cleaner appearance. She even paid for it and then bought me breakfast, too. Sure enough, when our train arrived at Borås, Sweden, Magda was at the train station waiting for me. She looked so pretty. We greeted each other with hugs and kisses. I felt comforted to be reconnected with her. We headed back to her apartment in her Volkswagen Bug.

CHAPTER **18** (1957)

SWEDEN

WHEN WE arrived at her home, Magda introduced me to her husband Meir and their son Jacob. Jacob was one-and-a-half years old. I gave them their gift of winter apples. Meir loved the apples and gobbled them up in no time.

Meir and I had great difficulty communicating orally with each other. He was from Poland and spoke six languages, but not Hungarian. However, because Meir had two deaf cousins, he knew about body language. So the two of us resorted to body language as our primary mode of communication.

The next day, our conversation led us to the Holocaust. We delicately shared the experiences. Magda was the interpreter. Magda shared very little of her experiences other than that which I already knew of becoming ill with tuberculosis in the camp. Meir explained that he had been in a concentration camp for five years and showed me the numbered tattoo that the Nazis had given him on his inner forearm for identification. He was the sole survivor of his immediate and extended families. In the camp, he had developed tuberculosis and would have to use medications for the rest of his life. Meir believed the Swedish government were miracle workers because they had been so helpful and good to him. By that time, the conversation had become quite painful, and we all agreed to not to share more tears. Consequently, I never was able to share my full experience.

During the first week of my stay, I wrote letters to my friends. One of them was Jenő Bátory, who was living in Copenhagen, Denmark. Jenő wasn't Jewish. However, he was a good friend of mine from the deaf club in Budapest. He was a leader in swimming. We had also been on the board together for the sports committee. The last time I had seen him was at the deaf club about the time of the Hungarian

In Borås, with my sister Magda and her one-and-a-half-year-old son Jacob.

Revolution. He responded quickly, being surprised to have received my letter.

Irén and Sándor sent me money for the first couple weeks until I was able to get on my feet. The money was also to help Magda and Meir because they had only enough income to support their daily living. I was surprised that Sándor was in Los Angeles, California, and I questioned Magda about it. Magda explained that Sándor's ship had docked somewhere in the Los Angeles area. He had had a layover and decided to visit Jolán. Jolán insisted that he stay put and not go back to the ship, so, Sándor stayed and lived with Jolán.

I decided to find the local deaf club. Meir searched around and found that one existed in Borås. Although Borås was a small and boring city, I went right away and immediately joined in the social activities. The deaf club became a way for me to pick up Swedish words quickly.

By the second week, I became restless staying in the apartment. I felt the need to do something with myself and the need to contribute to the family. I decided to look for a job. Meir assisted me because

I couldn't speak Swedish. I began searching throughout the city of Borås with no luck. I went to the deaf club, hoping to find out about job possibilities. The people at the deaf club said that jobs in Borås were hard to come by because Borås was primarily a textile town, and its workforce consisted primarily of women. It was estimated that the female workforce was at sixty-five percent! I realized that I had no choice but to look for a job out of town. Everyone at the deaf club advised me to go to Göteborg. They also suggested that I visit the Göteborg deaf club.

Shortly thereafter, I decided to head to Göteborg, the second largest city in Sweden, to check out the different factories. Meir did not assist me on this venture because he was ill. On a Friday morning at six o'clock, I boarded the train headed for Göteborg. The train ride lasted one hour, putting me there at seven o'clock. I exited the train and looked at my map to establish my bearings.

I decided to go to the ship factory, called Göta Verken. The people at the deaf club had recommended this place because it employed many deaf people. I was concerned about getting a job not only because I was deaf but also because I barely spoke Swedish. At the factory, the manager introduced himself. I explained that I was deaf and spoke only Hungarian. He decided to call over a hearing Hungarian employee to translate our conversation. We were able to communicate, which was wonderful. However, the factory had no job openings. But, he told me, go ahead and fill out an application, and if a job opening came up, he would let me know. I thanked him and the translator for their time and patience.

The translator accompanied me out of the factory, saying he had a referral that may lead me to other job possibilities. He gave me the address of an employment service. He said that the employment service had a department that specialized in services for deaf people. Without hesitation, I decided to go there next.

When I arrived at the employment service, I requested the department for deaf services. A woman approached me and began signing. I stopped her immediately and explained my limitations with the Swedish language. We decided to combine the methods, a little Swedish sign with speechreading and body language. We were then able to communicate at the minimal necessary level. She introduced herself as Mrs. Heden, from Stockholm. She asked me a little bit about my personal background and shared a bit of her own. She was hearing with deaf parents, which had led her to sign. She asked me whether I had any credentials. I showed her my mechanical diploma. She smiled and said she had the perfect job for me. She told me to wait while she placed a call to the Svenska Kullager Fabriken (SKF), or Sweden Ball Bearing Factory. The chief engineer of SKF told her to send me over immediately for an interview. She decided to accompany me to the interview as my interpreter.

When we arrived at SKF, the chief engineer welcomed us. He asked for my mechanical diploma. The engineer was very pleased with my credentials and hired me on the spot. I was happy and so was Mrs. Heden. One of the managers called in another deaf employee by the name of Fogel, who was a foreman. He was brought in to help our communication. Then, another employee, a woman, was called in. Fogel explained to me that the woman would assist me for the remainder of the day to purchase a work uniform, including a pair of shoes, and to get set up in a hotel, which was located approximately one kilometer from the factory. The hotel was actually owned by SKF, and the cost of the hotel would be deducted from my paycheck. I felt good inside that I had gotten a job.

The day was still young, so I decided to head downtown to check it out. I found it rather boring and, with the extra time I had, decided to check out the Göteborg deaf club. I hopped on a trolley car to get there. I figured out that to get from SKF to the club would take approximately half an hour. When I arrived, I found the club open, so I stayed until the early part of the evening. The deaf club offered social events, chess, bridge, and other card games. It had a rather large membership. I introduced myself to a few people, then left to return to Borås to tell Magda and Meir my wonderful news.

When I arrived home, Magda and Meir asked me about my day. I told them of my good fortune, and they were delighted. I couldn't believe that I had accomplished finding a job, a place to stay, and a social club all in one day. On Sunday evening, I left for Göteborg because I had to be at work at six o'clock in the morning. From this point on, my weekdays were spent in Göteborg, and my weekends were spent in Borås with Magda and her family.

Magda and Meir always included me in their weekend plans. One weekend, all of us were invited to a card party in Borås. Magda introduced me to her friend. She was an Austrian hearing woman. She wasn't Jewish, but she was married to a Polish Jew. She had met her husband in the hospital while she had been working as a nurse. He had been imprisoned for four years. After his camp was liberated, the Austrian woman had cared for him in the hospital. She fell in love with him, and after his recovery, they had wed. However, he had been unable to give his wife a baby. I believe she really loved her husband, but she longed for a baby. She felt like there was a void in her life, and from that night forward, she met me in secret to have sex. Looking back, I think she used me to try and get pregnant.

Eleven deaf people worked at the SKF factory. At break time, I conversed with them, which helped me improve my Swedish. The engineer was impressed by how quickly I was picking up the language and with my ability to work all the machines in the factory.

A couple months went by, and I knew my visa would soon expire. I was happy with my new life, and I wasn't prepared to go back to Budapest. In fact, I made a decision not to go back to Budapest, and that was that. I still had the dreams and visions of visiting western Europe, America, and Asia. I shared my dreams with Magda and Meir. They suggested that I apply for political asylum, which would allow me additional freedom.

Following their suggestion, I went to the Swedish police department and asked whether they could give me political asylum. All they could do was offer me a simple extension on my visa. I explained that an extension wouldn't serve my purposes. I pleaded with them, explaining that I had a job I was happy with and no family back in Budapest. They suggested that I apply for Swedish alien status. I didn't care what it took; I refused to be forced back to Budapest.

The application process for acceptance as a Swedish alien was extremely tedious. Meir had to help me fill out the forms. The questions were all in Swedish, and the technical ones were difficult for me to understand. The first question on the application was in reference to my name. It took the longest to answer because Meir thought that my first name, Imre, was not a good name and that I should change it. He conjectured that I needed a more neutral name if I were going to switch to a Swedish alien status. I couldn't grasp this concept. I only surmised that Meir was not fond of the Hungarian people or their country because of their wealth. The Hungarian arrivals in the camps apparently had been mean toward the Polish survivors, including Meir. The Hungarian Jews also had come into the camps healthy whereas the Poles suffered from malnutrition. In any case, I decided to go along with the name change as long as it would help me become a Swedish alien. Meir asked me whether I had another name I liked. The first one that came to mind was Chári, the nickname my family had called me when I was a child. Meir predicted that the Swedes wouldn't understand the name Chári. Trying again, I suggested the name Harry. This choice satisfied Meir.

From then on, my name became Harry Imre Dunai. I was surprised that my name change didn't require any official certification as it had when I changed my name back in Budapest. After that first transforming question, we moved on, filling out the remainder of the application. As soon as it was completed, I submitted it.

In the meantime, Jenő decided to come and visit me on a Friday at the hotel where I was staying. We chatted for a while about his escape through Austria during the Hungarian Revolution, fleeing directly to Denmark. The following day, we took the train to Borås to visit Magda and her family. Our communication process was very interesting. Jenő and I spoke in Hungarian Sign Language while I tried voicing simultaneously for Magda to hear. Magda did her best to translate my voiced Hungarian into voiced Swedish for Meir. Meir wanted to know exactly what Jenő and I were talking about. I assumed he wanted to be a part of our conversation and must have

During my visit with him in Copenhagen, Jenő Batory gave me the grand tour of the city.

felt left out. The following weekend, Meir told me that he understood how it felt to be left out of a conversation because during our conversation with Jenő, he had experienced not only a language barrier but also the barrier of my and Jenő's deafness. He mentioned that, if he had to choose, being deaf would be worse than being hearing with a language barrier.

After almost three weeks, I was finally granted Swedish alien status and received a Swedish passport. I was very happy because my dream to travel freely would soon become a reality. At the same time, I felt extremely guilty for betraying Mr. Kékési by not returning to Budapest.

With my new identity, I decided to take a two-day trip to Copenhagen, Denmark, to visit with Jenő. It would be a four-hour journey by train and ferry. I took a train from Göteborg to Malmö, then a ferryboat from Malmö to Copenhagen. When I arrived, Jenő was waiting for me, excited to see me. I stayed at his apartment in the heart of Copenhagen, where he resided alone. He gave me the grand tour of downtown Copenhagen, and naturally, we visited the deaf club. We also visited the King's Castle, learning that the king was a good man. He was successful in saving 8,000 of "his" Jews. It was a great couple of days.

After a couple more months went by, I could speak Swedish fluently. I picked up the language quickly from the employees at SKF, from the deaf club, from different girlfriends, and from Magda and

Dancing with a girl in Sweden in my tailored suit by Sam Fuch.

Meir. Being a part of the deaf club's chess team was an asset because communication was essential, so I was more motivated to learn. I also picked up the language by daily watching American cowboy movies that contained Swedish subtitles.

By the fall of 1957, Magda and Meir decided to move to Stockholm, Sweden. I continued to see them weekly, but now I traveled to Stockholm on the weekends. Irén continued to correspond with me from the United States. She sent me the Hungarian newspapers from California whenever she could. By now, she and Jolán had two sons each. I wondered to myself whether one day I would have a family. But for now, I was enjoying my new-found freedom.

I knew that Stockholm also had a deaf club, because our Göteborg chess team had played against their chess team. As soon as Magda and her family were settled in, I went to investigate that club. The club offered a fine program equal to that in Göteborg. While visiting there, I met a special girl. Her name was Kristina. She had blonde hair and blue eyes and was nicely built. Although I had other girlfriends, she became a steady girlfriend. My attraction for her was stronger than for the others. I kept in contact with Kristina during the weekdays while I worked in Göteborg. She helped me improve my Swedish. She also spoke English, which I found impressive.

CHAPTER 19 (1958)

THE LONDON CHESS TOURNAMENT

MY JOB WAS going very well. I was a mover and a shaker and quickly ascended up the ladder of the factory. SKF was providing me with a fully paid two-week vacation, which was nearing. I had made plans to go to London because the World Deaf Chess Tournament was to be held there. If it weren't for the tournament, I wouldn't have planned to go to London. I was looking forward to seeing my friends from Hungary who would be playing in the competition.

I went by train from Göteborg to Malmö, Sweden. On the train, I met a girl from Finland. As our eyes met, I sensed a feeling of powerful physical chemistry between us. Somehow or other, we met up in the hallway between the train cars where we began hugging and kissing each other. She stroked my face affectionately. I never felt my heart beat so hard with excitement. Unfortunately, her mother was watching us like a hawk. The train boarded the railroad ferry for Copenhagen, Denmark. In Copenhagen, I got off the ferry and said good-bye to the Finnish girl. Her train continued on to Germany. It was too bad. I wondered whether we could have had a relationship.

Jenő was there in Copenhagen to greet me for a brief one-hour interlude. From Copenhagen, I boarded a train that traveled to Rotterdam, Holland. In Rotterdam, the train boarded a huge ferry for the last leg of the journey before arriving in London.

On the ferry, I happened to meet a German deaf man, who was also headed to London for the chess tournament. We discovered that we would be staying in the same hotel. Throughout our journey, he boasted about Germany's qualities of health, science, and commodities. I let him rattle on because I was happy to have his companionship. The sea was extremely rough, and the man said that the conditions were typical for the North Sea. It was a blessing that the ferry was large and built to handle the rough conditions. I slept well. In the morning, we arrived at a port in England, then continued by train for London.

When I arrived in London, my friends from the Swedish chess team were there along with my friends from the Hungarian chess team. I was flooded with emotion to see my former Hungarian chess teammates. I wished I could play as part of their team, but I could attend the tournament only as a fan. I was unable to play on behalf of Hungary because I had forfeited my citizenship. I couldn't play for Sweden because I wasn't a citizen of Sweden, only an alien. I was, in fact, stateless. Regardless, I still enjoyed the tournament because I was with my friends.

After a few days at the tournament, I went to visit Charlotte. I couldn't figure out how to get to her place, so I decided to spend a little extra money and have a taxi driver figure it out for me. When I arrived, Charlotte had tears in her eyes. She was so pleased to see me, and I reciprocated her feelings. We spent hours discussing the past, the time spent apart, and what the future held. After our visit, I decided to try and take the subway back to my hotel. Charlotte gave me the proper directions. She also gave me directions to visit her aunt and uncle. The next day I went to see Aunt and Uncle Balkányi. They were happy to see me, too. They were now retired. I stayed for a couple of hours and joined them for tea. They wanted to know about my career and family.

The following day, I went to the London Jewish deaf club because the deaf community was supposed to be having a meeting. When I entered the club, I immediately set my eyes on one particularly well-endowed young lady. She was trying to help a little boy and was bending forward. When she looked up, she noticed that I was staring at her chest. She gave me the shame-shame-on-you sign with her fingers. She was also deaf, and her name was Jessica Rapaport. She was British-born. We used body language to communicate because I didn't know any English, and she didn't know Hungarian or Swedish. Although our languages differed, we nevertheless found ways to figure out our conversation.

Being that the deaf world can be a small world, Jessica started naming off people I might know. She began with the name Leslie Goldman. I told her that I knew a László Goldman. Wanting to know whether we were talking about the same person, she pulled a photograph of him out of her purse. We looked at each other, smiling and agreeing. I didn't know it at the time, but Jessica and Leslie were sweethearts. She named off a few more students who had originally come from eastern Europe, but I didn't know them.

Then came the grand-prize question: Did I know Charlotte Balkányi? I couldn't believe my eyes when she asked me that question. I was really shocked. I nodded yes with delight and didn't get a chance to explain how I knew Charlotte before Jessica began her story. Jessica explained in detail that Charlotte had been her teacher in London, at the Residential School for the Jewish Deaf and Dumb Children. She also described Charlotte as a woman in a mink coat with a cup of espresso and cigarette in hand, twenty-four hours a day, seven days a week. I laughed and agreed. I couldn't believe the coincidence. I excitedly told her that she had also been my teacher back in Budapest and that she was not known as Charlotte but as Sári néni. We both couldn't get over what a small world it was. Throughout our conversation, we found that we had more and more in common. We stayed until the club closed, and I accompanied her home by subway. She asked whether I wanted to meet her parents. I felt awkward; it was very late. We hugged and kissed each other good night.

It was such an amazing coincidence that Jessica and I had met. I could barely sleep that night. I decided I had to go back and visit Charlotte as soon as possible to tell her the news about Jessica. The next day, I showed up at Charlotte's door. She was pleasantly surprised to see me back so soon. I told her that I had met Jessica, which seemed to please her. She informed me that Jessica spoke well and could hear a good deal. She also told me that she liked Jessica very much. Charlotte's response meant a lot to me. We decided to plan an evening out with old friends from Budapest, including Jessica.

Everyone met up at Csárdás, a fine Hungarian restaurant in Pica-
dilly Circus. It was an evening to remember. Another Hungarian
friend of Charlotte's and mine treated Charlotte and Jessica to their
meals. A very nice hard-of-hearing man, who was a private student
of Charlotte's, also joined us. He apparently had good speech and
was beginning to master the English language. He was flirting with
Jessica, but I could tell she was not interested in him. After dinner, I
accompanied Jessica home. I declined to meet her parents once again
because the time was so late. Again, we hugged and kissed; Jessica was
very proper and would go no further.

Too soon, my trip had come to an end. I went to the train station
with my old Hungarian teammates and bid them farewell. I was surprised that Jessica came to the train station to say good-bye. Jessica
was a big help in assisting me with where I had to go and when I had
to board. She told me that I was in her heart. She made me make
a promise to write her letters. She was the first Jewish girl I had met
in whom I was actually interested.

MAKING PLANS FOR A NEW LIFE

ON THE WAY back to Sweden, I made another stopover in Copenhagen, meeting Jenő again. Jenő commented on my appearance, saying my face looked thinner. I figured it could have been from sleeping less and running around more. We spoke for about forty-five minutes before I had to board the ferry for Malmö. From the ferry, the train finally hooked up to a new engine and was now headed for Göteborg. I was exhausted and had to be at work the following morning. After work, I went to the deaf club to share my adventures in London.

That weekend, I visited with Kristina. I was happy to see her but realized I couldn't commit to any one woman. I never told any girlfriend, including Jessica and Kristina, that I had other girlfriends. Each girl believed she was the one and only.

The following week, I received a four-page letter from Jessica. I tried extremely hard to translate the letter from English to Swedish, but it was an arduous task. Finally, I had to ask my Hungarian hearing friend who spoke English to translate the letter for me. I responded to Jessica's four-page letter with a single page of only two sentences, even though I wished I could express more. Jessica continued to write lengthy letters, and my responses continued to be limited to a few words. I also shared Jessica's letters with Magda and Meir. They knew that Jessica was my first serious relationship with a Jewish girl.

I knew that I needed to learn English. Initially, I purchased the *World Times* magazine, hoping to pick up the language quickly. But English was very difficult to grasp. I wrote a letter to Péter in Budapest, requesting that he mail me a dictionary that would translate English to Hungarian and Hungarian to English. During the interim, I began learning English through children's books that were in Swedish and had English translations. Finally, I received the dictionaries from Péter. He had not been able to find a dictionary that combined word translations from English to Hungarian and from Hungarian to English, so he had to send two separate dictionaries instead. I began building my vocabulary quickly, at a rate of nearly five words per day.

By that time, I was back to my old routine—working during the week and visiting Magda and her family on the weekend. I was back

My old friend Péter Faragó sent dictionaries from Hungary to help me learn the English language.

at the deaf club, too, playing chess, bridge, and table tennis. In fact, I got a bridge contract to play in Göteborg and Stockholm.

I was still involved with other girls, but Kristina was the main girl in my life. I was in love with her, but I constantly had Jessica in the back of my mind. At the same time, I was getting tired of juggling the other girls. On a typical weekend, I saw three girls in one day, for example, one girl from eight in the morning till noon, another from noon until four, then the last one from five till nine. None of them ever knew I was such a playboy. However, I did care for each of them in some way. Maybe, I was searching for love and comfort that I missed as a child, or maybe my compulsiveness for these girls was simply a normal developmental stage.

In the fall of 1958, I decided that I was ready to see America. It seemed as though most of my family had moved west. Sándor, Irén, and Jolán had established residency in Los Angeles, California. And although Salgo and Lenke were still in Komjata, I knew that one day, they, too, would end up in Los Angeles.

I discussed my move to America with Magda and Meir. Meir preferred that I move to Israel, and Magda remained neutral. However, they agreed that they wanted me to be happy with whatever decision I made. Anticipating the future, I thought it would be wise to file for an immigration visa, so I went to the American Embassy in Stockholm.

The American Embassy said I had to follow a list of procedures. Naturally, it began with a cumbersome questionnaire. Aside from the endless questions on the application, however, I faced a quota issue. America had a quota on how many immigrants it would allow into the country. For me, the quota was a blessing. Because my origin of birth was in Czechoslovákia, my waiting period would be only three to six months. If I'd been born in Hungary, the wait could have been as long as three to five years. The approval process also required that I have a complete health exam. This exam included chest X rays for tuberculosis, a number of immunizations, and a check for venereal disease. The embassy also had to conduct a background search, checking police reports for any criminal activity. Once all the steps were completed, I simply had to wait.

Four or five months went by, and I hadn't received any word from the embassy. I didn't know what the holdup was. I waited another two months, and then I wrote a letter to Irén and Jolán, explaining that nothing was being done. In response, Irén and Jolán wrote a letter on my behalf to the American Embassy, pushing them along. Apparently, immigrants needed guaranteed proof of financial support. Irén and Jolán provided the necessary proof to satisfy the financial requirement. Sándor could not provide it, because he was not yet an American citizen. During this period, the waiting was nerve-racking.

I calculated that, by the month of July, my immigration visa should arrive. I wanted desperately to begin my tour of western Europe, Israel, and then America, but I felt that I was in a pickle. If I left prematurely, I may miss receiving my visa to go to America. I decided to go the American Embassy in Stockholm. Meir decided to accompany me to the embassy, and together, we explained my dilemma to them. They said they could send my visa to any country in the world that had an American Embassy and that sending it to Israel would be no problem. Their suggestion was a fantastic alternative, and I was satisfied. Nevertheless, I remained concerned about timing. The embassy insisted that everything would work out, and they guaranteed that I would receive approval when I arrived in Israel. Although, I was a bit skeptical, I began mapping out my travel plans.

By May 1959, I told the chief engineer at SKF that I was planning to tour Western Europe and then go to America. The engineer fully understood my position of wanting to go and told me that, if I were unhappy in America, I would always have a job waiting for me at the factory. I felt special and relieved to know that, if I didn't like America, I could come back and have a job waiting.

I bought the necessary tickets and obtained my itinerary for western Europe, Israel, New York, and ultimately, Los Angeles, California. The entire trip would take two months. As I made the arrangements, Magda got word that Sándor was marrying a nice Jewish American girl whose name was Esther. It was exciting news. In contrast, I said good-bye to Kristina. She was heartbroken, and I felt bad for leaving her. Oddly though, I didn't feel crushed. I told her that I would write to her, and she agreed to correspond.

All of my friends questioned me as to why I wanted to go to America. From my heart, I told them that I wanted to see the world, that I loved traveling, that I was interested in other cultures, and that I missed my family. They didn't believe me, saying that I was blinded by the almighty American dollar.

CHAPTER 21 (1959)

FAREWELL TO SWEDEN AND ONWARD TO EUROPE AND ISRAEL

SOON, I WOULD be saying farewell to Sweden. Two weeks before I was to leave, I gave up my job and hotel and went to live in Stockholm. I wanted to spend quality time with Magda and her family before departing. Magda and Meir told me that the Austrian woman was pregnant. Meir suspected it was my child. Later though, when the baby was born, Magda sent me a letter saying that the baby was the husband's because it looked like him. I will never know for sure, and it doesn't matter because she bore the baby she longed for. When the time came to go, I had difficulty saying good-bye to Magda and her family and to my friends at the deaf club. Magda and Kristina both bid me farewell at the train station.

My trip began by staying with Jenő in Denmark for two days. I knew it would be a while before I'd see him again. From Copenhagen, Denmark, I boarded a ferry headed for Hamburg, Germany. The highlight on board was the seafood, which was excellent. From Hamburg, Germany, I boarded a train to Paris, France.

When I arrived in Paris, I went directly to my hotel. Then, immediately consulted my World Deaf Club Directory and went to find the local deaf club.

At the French deaf club, the members asked where I was from. When they found out I was Hungarian, they said they had a good-sized membership of Hungarians and that all the Hungarians hung out at the local coffee shop. I stayed for a brief period, then headed to the coffee shop. There, I met up with a man named Mr. Grunfeld. He was from Budapest and had been a student at my institute, but he had left the school just as I had enrolled. He recommended that I go and see the Follies, the museums, and other city highlights. I asked him whether he knew a man named Imre Bokor because I had suspected Imre had moved to Paris. Mr. Grunfeld replied that he knew him very well. Simultaneously, we signed to each other, saying Imre was "the smart and intelligent one." Then, we both nodded and laughed.

Mr. Grunfeld offered me Imre's address while expressing his complaints about the man. He said that Imre criticized French people, telling them they were uneducated and low class and adding any other put-down he could think of. Apparently, Imre felt superior because of his fantastic command of the French language. I was astounded that Imre, although deaf, could grasp the language without ever being taught French! I listened to everything that Mr. Grunfeld had to say, then thanked him and left.

The next day, I went to visit Imre. He did not know I was coming. His apartment was on the fifth floor, the roof level, because the rent there was cheapest. The building had no elevators, so the rent was lower at each higher floor. I knocked and rang his doorbell. Imre opened the door slowly, peeking his head out. He stared at me, wondering who I was. Quickly, I said, "Hello. I'm Izráel Deutsch." "Oh my God!" he said excitedly. "I remember you. I've thought of you often."

Imre invited me in. We immediately began discussing what had happened to him back in Budapest because we had spent time together in the Red Cross camp. But, at some point, when the Arrow Cross soldiers were dividing us up by age and so forth, I didn't see Imre around. At the time, I figured he had been taken to a camp or shot along the way. So Imre explained his story. He had been on a trolley car returning to the Red Cross camp when he saw the Arrow Cross troops dividing everyone up. He decided to stay on the trolley car, riding to the edge of town and becoming a fugitive. There, he went into hiding, and later, he fled to France.

Our visit was truly a heartfelt reunion for us. We spent our time discussing politics; Imre claimed he was a Communist. Unfortunately, he wasn't happy with the way that Russia was handling matters and, during our discussion, tore up his communist book. I shared that I agreed with him.

When I left, I found myself craving Hungarian food. I looked through the phone book to find a Hungarian restaurant and was successful. At the restaurant, the woman manager noticed that I was deaf and Hungarian. She asked whether I knew Imre. I nodded yes. She told me that Imre was a bad boy, a dedicated gambler, betting at the horse races on a regular basis. She also said he was a regular customer. After her commentary, she served me dinner. I wanted to savor each bite because the food was so good. The French food had been a bit too heavy for me. I was used to eating the lighter food back in Sweden.

I went back to my hotel and changed my clothing so I could go to the Folies-Bergère. The dress code required a suit and tie. The show was three hours long and incredibly beautiful. However, it was no match for the Follies in Las Vegas, Nevada, of today. After the show, I went back to the hotel for the night.

The next morning, I toured the various sights that Imré and Mr. Grunfeld had recommended. I also went to visit Charlotte's parents. Father Balkányi could no longer speak, and his family had to read his lips. I didn't know what was wrong with him, but he'd had some sort of throat surgery, and a tube now stuck out of his throat. I visited with the Balkányis for a short afternoon tea and pastry.

After staying in Paris for five days, I headed for Vienna, Austria. I boarded the train in Paris and made a two-hour layover at the border town of Basel, Switzerland. I decided to go out and have lunch at the train station. Off in the distance, I could smell the scents of goulash and rye bread. I followed the aroma to a Hungarian restaurant and decided to dine there. The food tasted great—authentic Hungarian.

After lunch, I reboarded the train. The journey was exhausting. When I arrived at the train station in Vienna, Austria, my cousin, Isek Mermelstein, also from Komjata, was waiting for me. Isek recognized me immediately. However, I didn't recognize him because he was much older than I. When we arrived at his home, he introduced me to his wife and two children. During my stay, we discussed the family very little. Isek did mention, however, that before the war, he had tried to persuade Salgo to flee to Paris with him. But Salgo felt the need to go home after being in the camp.

Isek's wife tried to keep me entertained. She took me sightseeing for several days. We visited a large castle in Vienna, took several walks in different parks, and we even went to see some Roman Catholic churches. Isek was unable to accompany us because he was extremely busy at work.

Isek and his family were very religious. Isek told me that from Friday evening through Saturday evening, I was not to touch the electricity. His electricity functioned by an automatic timer. The strictness reminded me of my days on the farm.

Isek owned a textile factory. I was interested in his operation, so he gave me a tour. It was a large factory that produced different types of fabric. Afterwards, he took me out to help me purchase a new camera called a Pentax. My plan was to sell the camera in Israel.

Alone, I visited the Vienna deaf club. I ran into some non-Jewish friends whom I knew from the deaf club in Budapest. I was very happy to see them. They had fled Budapest during the Hungarian Revolution when the borders had opened up. We communicated with ease. In fact, I was also able to communicate with the deaf Austrians. The sign language at the club was very similar to Hungarian sign language because of the proximity of the countries, even though the spoken languages differed greatly.

For entertainment, I decided to go to the circus. To get there, I had to cross a bridge over the Danube River. As I walked over the bridge looking down at the Danube River, I was overcome with emotion. The course of the river took it to Budapest, and at that moment, it took me back to my childhood memories. I just wanted to fall into the water because I felt terribly homesick. Trying to change my thoughts, I quickly walked on to the circus. The circus was festive and enjoyable, but the aroma of the food in the circus tent made me think of having Hungarian food again. After the circus, I went searching for another Hungarian restaurant. I was unsuccessful and went back to Isek's home. Isek's wife was a good cook, so I settled for her meals instead. Unlike the French food, the Austrian food was tastier and easier to digest.

The next day, I walked around Vienna, touring the different museums. The history of Vienna was very interesting and was very similar to that of Budapest. After visiting with family and friends as well as seeing the sites, my time in Vienna came to an end. Isek accompanied me back to the train station where I boarded the train for Rome, Italy. We crossed over the Italian border sometime about midmorning. The train's customs agent was checking everyone's visas. I gave him mine, and he shook his finger, indicating no. He pointed to the date on the visa, which showed that the visa would expire the following day. My mind began racing, and my body tightened from anxiety, thinking of the worst possible scenarios. I wondered why things in my life were always so complicated. Luckily, the situation was not as bad as I thought. The customs man asked me how long I planned to stay in Italy and the reason for my visit. I told him that I was staying for five days and then was headed for Israel. He said that he would issue an extension on my visa for a small fee. So I paid the fee and got the extension. I felt a great sense of relief.

When I arrived in Rome, I checked into a hotel. My plan was to stay for a couple of days. I visited the Roman Colosseum and other ruins, but my visit to the Vatican was a treat. It was incredibly beautiful. The rooms in the Vatican explained the history of the Pope, and they were full of oil paintings, jewelry, diamonds, and other precious stones that were priceless gems, probably the richest in the world.

Naturally, I decided to visit the deaf club. Again, the communication at the club was fine, and the members enjoyed my company. They wanted me to join their group on a mountain hike, but I had to decline because it didn't fit into my itinerary. They asked me whether I was Italian. I told them that I was from Sweden. They all laughed at me in disbelief because my coloring did not seem to suggest a Swedish background. I had to explain what my roots were. They seemed very interested about my history.

The following morning, I hopped on another train to Naples. I stayed in a hotel for three days. In Naples, I found another deaf club, which was run by the Catholic community. The priest was the club's organizer and leader. I played chess against him and beat him— twice. The mountain and ocean views from Naples were incredibly intense and beautiful. I had heard that Naples was famous for thieves who robbed tourists, but I didn't worry because I felt that I fit in, looking Italian myself.

My time was now coming to an end in western Europe. I decided to head down toward the port earlier than I had planned. All passengers were required to be on board the ship by two o'clock in the afternoon. As soon as I arrived at the port, my belly began growling. I could smell stuffed bell peppers, one of my favorite dishes. Like a detective, I tracked down the smell to a boat named *Theodor Herzl*, the very boat that I needed to board to go to Israel. I had gone without stuffed bell peppers for three years in Sweden. Now, I'd be eating stuffed peppers on my way to Israel!

The *Theodor Herzl* would be carrying five hundred passengers. I went to the registration desk and presented my ticket. A chaperone escorted me to my cabin just below the main deck. I was delighted to have a window in my room because I could see the ocean. The room held a bunk bed, and I took the bottom bunk. I never saw my roommate. Before leaving, my escort gave me a program of the activities on board.

I took my own tour of the boat to become acclimated. The ship offered dinner groups, which were scheduled in two shifts, six o'clock and eight o'clock. I selected the six o'clock group. At dinner, I got what I had been hoping for—stuffed bell peppers. They tasted as if they came directly from Hungary.

During dinner, I saw a girl with her mother. The girl looked just like Jessica, which made me curious. I approached her and asked where she was from. Coincidentally, she, too, was from London, England. The girl smiled at me, and her mother took notice, watching over us like a protective mother bear. I didn't bother pursuing her after that.

Aboard the *Theodor Herzl* on the way to Israel.

The ship was like a village on the water. The trip to the port in Haifa, Israel, took two and a half days, so I spent the time playing table tennis, cards, and bridge.

When I arrived in Israel, my cousin, Naftali Deutsch, was waiting for me. He was wearing a police uniform. He told me that I would not to have to go through customs because he was the chief of police in Tel Aviv. He told me that I would be staying with him and his family. We boarded a beautiful German-made train and headed off for a one-hour ride to his home. I stayed with Naftali, his wife Hanka, his ten-year-old daughter Orella, and their dog for three weeks.

During my stay, I went to the Tel Aviv deaf club. The actual name of the club was the Helen Keller Deaf Club. While there, I met up with my former classmates from the institute, Hermann Zoldán and Ernö Rosenblüth. We spent hours discussing our school days, the war, and current events. It was an emotional time for the three of us.

I decided that I should take advantage of sightseeing during my stay in Israel. Naftali suggested that sightseeing was best by joining a tour group. He booked me a package deal with three other American tourists. The tour package was a good deal because, as a group, we could split the costs. My group drove together to Jerusalem at the Jordanian border. We couldn't go to the Western Wall because it was located in eastern Jerusalem and was occupied by the Arabs. That was okay because we were able to see Jerusalem's fabulous museum depicting the city's history.

From there, we drove to Be'er Sheva, located in the desert. We went to see it for two reasons. It was en route to our final destination of the Dead Sea, and it was a newly developed city. We toured the new city and had lunch at a restaurant. The day was extremely hot, with the temperature at approximately forty-five degrees Celsius.

After lunch, we headed to the Dead Sea, which has the lowest sea level on earth. The Dead Sea is a wonderful quirk of nature. The salt content is so high that a person cannot drown. I entered the sea and stayed afloat. We were told not to stay in the water too long because we could easily get sunburned. It was late in the evening when we

In Tel Aviv, I met up with my classmates from the institute. Back row, from left to right, Andor Kaufmann, Lászlo Goldman, Sándor Katz, Lázár Perl, Hermann Zoldán, Ferenc Ehrenfeld. Front row, left to right, Judit Teichmann, Éva Csányi, Mrs. Ehrenfeld, Szerán Feuer, me, Rózsi Iczkovics.

arrived back in Tel Aviv. Throughout the wonderful tour, my mind kept wandering off, thinking about the status of my visa. I was feeling very restless.

The next morning, Naftali decided to accompany me to Haifa, where I would be staying with Meir's cousin for three days. I don't remember Meir's cousin's name, but his last name was also Rosenberg. Anyway, Naftali had met their family before and wanted to visit them again. When we arrived in Haifa, Rosenberg and his family greeted us warmly. Naftali was satisfied getting caught up with whatever news he needed to discuss, and that evening, he went back to Tel Aviv. Rosenberg had a wife, a son, and a daughter. I remember only that their son's name was Ábrahám. Ábrahám spoke English fluently and was studying to become a doctor. While staying with them, he took me to see the Golan Heights near the Syrian border. We also took a tour of a kibbutz and explored the city of Haifa.

After my great stay, I went back alone to Tel Aviv by train. As soon as I returned to Naftali's place, Naftali took me to the American Embassy to find out about the status of my immigration visa. The embassy in Israel telephoned the American Embassy in Stockholm, Sweden. The visa approval had been processed and was supposedly being mailed directly to Naftali's home. On the journey back to Naftali's home, I felt a sense of relief knowing the visa approval would arrive soon.

During the next few days, I visited with friends at the deaf club. Finally, a letter arrived saying that I could pick up my visa at the embassy. I was expecting the visa to arrive at Naftali's home. In any case, I was glad it had arrived. I went back to the embassy and obtained the necessary visa stamp. I also sold my Pentax camera to a friend whom Naftali knew. With the money I made, I bought silver platters to give to Jolán, Irén, and Sándor, as gifts for when I arrived in America.

During my stay, László Goldman and his parents invited me for dinner. I learned that László was, in fact, Jessica's childhood sweetheart. Charlotte had set up Jessica and László as pen pals back in 1952 and they had been staying in touch for seven years. We agreed that

While in Tel Aviv, I visited my old classmate László Goldman and his family and found out that he and Jessica were childhood sweethearts.

Jessica was definitely friendly and flirtatious. Although the evening was pleasant, I found myself thinking more and more about leaving for America.

Each day was filled with major social events with friends or family. On one occasion, I was asked to give a lecture at the deaf club, discussing the deaf cultures of Budapest and Sweden. I willingly obliged. I was even asked whether I was interested in being introduced to a nice Jewish deaf girl. I declined the offer.

A couple of days before my stay in Israel ended, Naftali told me that his neighbor had a daughter who was going to America and who was leaving on the same day, at the same time, and on the same boat, which was called *Jerusalem.* He took me to meet her and her family. She was a nice Israeli, Jewish, hearing woman, probably about twenty-four years old, just a bit younger than I was. I think Naftali and her parents were hoping that we'd keep each other company on board the ship. On the day of my departure, Naftali and his family accompanied me to the port along with the girl and her family. We all said our farewells.

Leaving Israel from the port in Haifa, I boarded the beautiful German-made ship, *Jerusalem,* to New York. The ship was slightly larger than the *Herzl.* The ship departed, heading through the Mediterranean Sea. En route, we had a two-hour cargo layover in Naples, Italy, but all passengers had to stay aboard ship. We then made another stopover in Gibraltar, which was under British control, even though it was a Spanish colony. There, we were allowed to disembark for three-quarters of a day.

Not being able to find the Israeli woman, I spent the day touring the city with an American hearing girl I had met on board the ship. Back aboard, I danced, ate, drank, and played chess, bridge, and table tennis. I wrote on pieces of paper as best I could in English to communicate with the other passengers. The Israeli girl who boarded the ship with me was spending her time with a group she connected with. I was also not attracted to her. So whenever our paths crossed, we simply said hello to each other.

One of the highlights of my voyage was when I was invited to the captain's table for dinner. The captain selected passengers from various countries to dine with him on a nightly basis. I felt very honored. Most of the passengers I sat with that evening were Americans who were returning from trips to Israel. However, I also met another Hungarian man who told me not to worry about getting a job in America. He explained that my mechanical degree was equivalent to an engineering degree in the United States. In addition, America was lacking people with technical skills and abilities. Getting that information helped my confidence.

Approximately on the eighth day of my voyage, a terrible hurricane-like storm fell on us in the middle of the Atlantic Ocean. Many people became seasick, displaying their pale, drawn faces. I began feeling queasy myself and went to my cabin. I couldn't shake the nausea, and decided that maybe the pool would help me. I put on my swim trunks and headed for the pool deck.

The minute I got in the pool, I felt a hundred percent better. The motion of the water in the pool seemed to offset the rough conditions of the ocean. I gestured to the other passengers to join me, trying to tell them that the pool was helping my nausea. One by one, passengers entered the pool, but for some, the therapy came too late to soothe them.

After a voyage of fifteen days, the ship came to port in New York on July 31, 1959. The time had gone by amazingly fast. I was never lonely on board. As we entered the port, the faces of everyone on board were awestruck. I followed their gazes toward the enormous Statue of Liberty. I couldn't believe what I was seeing. Most of us had never seen such an incredible, enormous structure, especially from on board a ship and up close.

CHAPTER **22** (1959)

AMERICA AND THE ANGEL IN THE SKY

AS WE LEFT the ship, everyone was required to go through customs. The process was extremely long, and it involved having to show all my documentation, including my medical records and X rays. First, customs reviewed all my possessions in a separate room. They told me I had to pay a fee for the silverware I had purchased in Israel. I told them that they were gifts for my family. They decided to waive the fee. Then, they sent me to the Immigration Health Department room. Here, they reviewed my medical records and X rays. Then, wishing me luck in America, they stamped my passport.

Another one of Meir's cousins was waiting for me at the customs exit. I stayed in New York with him and his family for one week. I found it easy to maneuver through the city with a map. I traveled by bus and the subway. During one of my forays, I went to Brooklyn to visit my old schoolmate, Márkus Kohn. When I got there, his mother said he was out. I never met up with him but, later, learned he had mental health problems.

Meir's cousin took me around the city of New York where we saw Times Square and went to a show at a theater. I was amazed by all the people of different nationalities and couldn't stop staring at everyone, especially the black people. I recalled reading newspaper reports in Budapest about how black people were treated poorly by the white people. I felt sympathy toward them because I knew what hatred was all about.

I also decided that, while I was in New York, I should visit a man named Henry Feldman. My friends from the Stockholm deaf club had told me he had been a student in Budapest at the institute. They had given me his address, and I was curious to meet him. When I arrived at his apartment, his deaf American wife answered the door. She told me he was at work and gave me his business address. I left immediately to find Henry. As I approached the address, I could see nothing but jewelry stores. I entered the business and asked for Henry. He replied that he was Henry. I began talking to him in Hungarian, explaining that I was a student from the institute in Budapest and that my friends from the Stockholm deaf club had given me his name and address.

He was very excited that I had come to visit him. We sat down over coffee and pastry and began discussing the institute days and the events of the war. Henry had left the institute in 1938, which was one year before I had entered the school. He had been sent to a concentration camp. Surviving the camp, the Red Cross shipped him off to Sweden, just like they had done for my sisters. We also discussed America. I was curious to know how he got himself into the jewelry business. His response was a rich wife and rich in-laws. His in-laws had bought him the business that he was now running. When I told him of my plan to go to Los Angeles, California, he said that Los Angeles was boring. In his opinion, California was a bunch of farms and cows. New York was the place to be, according to Henry. I was amused because he had never been to California. He had only heard about the place. Although the visit was interesting, we made no plans to meet again, but I told him that, if I visited New York in the future, I'd stop by.

My stay in New York had rushed by, and unfortunately, I had no time left to check out the New York deaf club. I sent a telegram to Irén in California with my estimated time of arrival at the airport. I was to fly for the first time in my life—on a brand-new Boeing 707 jet! The day we were to leave, it was raining heavily. Nevertheless, the plane was scheduled to take off despite the conditions. I boarded the plane, feeling excited and nervous. As we lifted off, I personally named our plane the "Angel in the Air." I was still concerned about the poor weather conditions. But as soon as we rose above the rain-filled clouds, the weather was perfect. For the first time, I could see puffy white clouds up close. The scene could have been heaven. I not only had a heavenly window view but also an attractive woman sitting next to me. We wrote notes to each other. I told her it was my first flight and described my feelings about the beauty of the sky. She acknowledged my thoughts. The airline provided us with lunch, and together we indulged in a few spirits.

When I arrived at the Los Angeles Airport, nobody was there to greet me. I went directly to the baggage claim to pick up my suitcases. Again, I looked around for my family but could see no one. Spotting the information desk, I went there and explained my dilemma. I asked the agent if he would call Irén, writing down my request in English along with Irén's phone number. He obliged and proceeded to dial her number. Irén answered the phone, and the agent read the paper to Irén. Irén told the man in Hungarian that she would pick me up in half an hour. The man tried to relate the words in Hungarian to me. It was quite funny. Irén was unaware that I could speak some English.

Eventually, Irén arrived alone. Our reunion was not outwardly dramatic, even though we hadn't seen each other in fifteen years. But inwardly, I was overcome with emotion to finally see her. I immediately asked her whether she had received my telegram. She said she hadn't. (To our amusement, it would arrive the next day—a waste of money, however.) We got into her 1950s model Chevrolet and took the side streets all the way to her home.

When we arrived at Irén's home, her three sons, Harvey, Manny, and Arthur, were there to greet me. After chatting for several hours, Irén's husband, Sam, came home from work. He and I chatted while Irén prepared dinner. Sam's aunt was also at their home because she usually baby-sat the three boys.

Later that evening, Sándor (who now went by the name Tuli) as well as Jolán and Aron plus their two sons, Harry (today known as Chaim Yitzchok) and Mickey, came to visit. Our conversations in Hungarian continued for many hours. The family gathering seemed odd to me, however. Everyone appeared to have a "normal" life. I felt a bit out of place. Among themselves, they all seemed like a family, but I had not lived with them for at least fifteen years and did not feel that I was a part of it.

A couple of days later, Jolán and her family took me to Disneyland. It was a fantastic fairyland. I was awed that everything was so incredible, costly, and beautiful. I turned to Aron and told him that the American dollar seemed almost equal to God. He was appalled by my comment and told me never to make a remark like that again. At first, I figured he didn't want me to say that because it was an insult to the American people. But he really meant that my comment was an insult to God. This conversation brought me back to my days in Sweden when my friend accused me of being blinded by the American dollar. In any case, I dropped the subject with Aron. Still, the Disney experience was so great that I wrote to all my friends in Europe, including Jessica, to tell them of my experience.

When I arrived back at Irén's house, Sam and I sat down for an in-depth discussion about politics. I made a reference about niggers. Sam immediately stopped me dead in the middle of my sentence and said that the word *nigger* was an insulting and inappropriate word. In America, he added, I should use the terms *black people* or *colored people*. I was surprised because, throughout Europe, *nigger* was the acceptable word. Regardless, I accepted the new terminology because I wanted to be correct and respectful.

Tuli eventually took me to his home to meet his wife, Esther. They had been married only four months. When I arrived, she was resting in bed. She had suffered a miscarriage. Nevertheless, Esther went out of her way to make me feel comfortable. She was a great hostess, and I liked her American style. Plus, she was very classy. I had dinner with the both of them plus Esther's sister. Surprisingly, Esther had no idea that I was deaf. Tuli never had felt it necessary to tell her.

A few days later, I found out that Esther and her sister had had a talk with Irén about me. Irén loved being a matchmaker. Apparently, Esther's sister thought I was handsome. I was honored, but I told Irén that I didn't want a hearing woman. I needed a deaf one. I decided to tell Irén that I had met a Jewish girl in London, England, named Jessica. I also informed her that Jessica and I had been writing letters to each other since my visit to London. Irén was happy and excited for me. I didn't tell her about Kristina, because of Kristina's religious background. I didn't want to hurt Irén's feelings. However, Magda knew about Kristina, so maybe Irén had heard about Kristina anyway. In any case, Irén never asked about her.

A few days later, I realized that to get around and survive in California, I would need a vehicle. Unfortunately, California didn't have a very good transportation system as did Europe and New York. But first, I had to learn to drive. I took a five-hour, private driver-education class. In addition, Sam and Tuli spent time teaching me on the side. Being a quick learner, I passed the written driver's license exam and received a learner's permit just after taking the course. Two weeks later, I received my driver's license.

Meanwhile, Irén had not given up on her matchmaking. She and her family had been invited to a bar mitzvah for her friend's son and decided to include me. Irén wanted to set me up with her friend's husband's cousin, who was a deaf girl from Pittsburgh. As soon as we got there, Jolán and Irén quickly introduced me to the girl. I don't remember her name, but I do recall that she was from a very wealthy family and that her father owned a butcher shop in Pittsburgh. She and I spoke at length during the party, had good communication, and enjoyed our time together. After the bar mitzvah, Aron prodded me to marry the girl because she had a wealthy family. I had to tell Aron that I wasn't interested in her money and that she was not in my heart. I didn't make any promises to the girl, although I believe she was hoping that I would write to her in Pittsburgh. I never did because I didn't want to give her any false hopes.

A week or so later, Irén decided to take me to an ear doctor. She wanted me to have an ear operation. The doctor said that an operation would be too risky at my age. In another attempt to help me regain my hearing, Irén bought me a hearing aid with a large battery. She also paid for me to have speech therapy at the University of California, Los Angeles. After a few weeks of failure, I gave up. I was unable to pick up any sounds and became frustrated with the whole process.

I soon found out about a deaf club in the heart of downtown Los Angeles, known as Los Angeles Club for the Deaf, or LACD. I joined their chess club and eventually became their champion. Many women at the club were interested in me; however, even though I dated a few of them, I made it perfectly clear that I had a girlfriend living in England.

Now, I wanted and needed a job. I told Irén and Sam I wanted to find a job working with the turret. Nobody knew what turret meant, and we spent quite a bit of time trying to translate the word into one we could all understand. Finally, we determined that the turret had something to do with an engine lathe. Irén, Sam, and Tuli finally could point me in the proper direction.

I checked out various jobs in the machining industry. I couldn't do plumbing work because I lacked fluency in English and did not have a plumber's license. The pay for the machining industry was surprisingly low. I thought about the man on the voyage from Israel to New York. He had told me that I'd have no problems getting a job. The requirement for most of the job advertisements listed was that the applicant possess his own tools. I didn't have any. The American firms weren't interested in my diploma; they were more interested in how I could perform.

I finally found a job with a starting pay of one dollar and fifty cents per hour. I agreed to take it because I decided that something was better than nothing. I knew I had to prove myself. My decision paid off because, by the end of my first day of work, I was given a twenty-five cent raise. My new employer acknowledged that I was able to do a variety of tasks.

Now that I had a job, I could focus on two other goals: improving my English and buying a car. I challenged myself to engage in as many conversations as possible so I would have to practice my new language. At the same time, I proudly bought my first car, a Pontiac Bonneville, for six hundred dollars. It was a dark pumpkin color with white-rimmed wheels. And, it was a gas-guzzler.

My employer was very satisfied with my performance and encouraged me to work as much overtime as I could. I realized that he was taking advantage of my lower pay rate; all the other employees were making two dollars and fifty cents per hour or more. But I

My first car was a pumpkin-colored Pontiac Bonneville with whitewall tires.

accepted the overtime because it would help me pay my debts, save money, and pay for gasoline. Gasoline prices were approximately fifteen to twenty cents per gallon.

Even though I was satisfied with my job, I continued searching for other jobs with better pay. Every week, I purchased the newspaper called the *Magyar Sag,* which was published in Hungarian. One day, in the advertisement section, I found an announcement for a machinist at a factory called Fibreform Electronics. The job was advertised with a starting pay of two dollars and seventy-five cents per hour. I decided to check it out. Sam decided to accompany me to the factory.

At Fibreform Electronics, the foreman, Art, expressed an interest in me. I had filled out an application, including a comment about my interest and skills in table tennis. Art, Sam, and I engaged in a long conversation and found that we shared a lot in common. Art's mother was from Budapest. Meanwhile, Art's boss, Bob, reviewed my application and then invited me to play some table tennis on the spot. Sam and Art continued to talk while I played. After the game,

Bob told me that I was hired but that my starting pay would be twenty-five cents less per hour than the advertised price because I had no tools. I went to my job the next day and gave notice, telling them I had another job for better pay. They were disappointed and offered to pay me the same amount Fibreform had guaranteed me. I declined their offer.

I could tell that Bob wanted to get to know me. He invited me to his home for dinner, and I accepted his invitation. We sat that evening, eating, drinking, and of course, playing table tennis afterwards. His hospitality amazed me. In Europe, my bosses generally had kept me at arm's length. I had felt the boundary between their level and mine. Yet, here in America, I found the bosses to be friendly. Soon, I began going to Bob's home every Thursday after work, along with Art and another one of Bob's friends who was a salesman. We typically ate dinner together and then played table tennis.

After a few weeks, Art offered me the option of deducting five dollars per week from my paycheck so I could slowly build up my own supply of tools. I thought it was a good idea and accepted the offer. Art was extremely pleased with my performance. He was also proud because I was Hungarian and he was half Hungarian. The two of us played table tennis during every break and sometimes after our workday ended.

Unfortunately, after a few months, Art had to lay me off because of a lack of work. I began to search for a new job, but all of the places where I applied were not interested in me because I was not an American citizen. I began to feel that I was a nobody. The feeling was not new to me. I knew I had to forge ahead.

Finally, I came across another advertisement for a machinist, in the *Los Angeles Times* classified section. I went to the location, arriving before eight o'clock in the morning because that is how I liked to operate. The secretary gave me an application. I refused to fill it out, telling the secretary that I wanted a simple yes or no answer whether I could have the job. The secretary called the foreman in to meet with me. I presented the foreman with my previous employer's name and phone number. The foreman phoned Art, and I was hired on the spot. The foreman told me that Fibreform gave me high marks. After I got the good news, I went ahead and filled out the application. I was offered twenty cents more per hour to work the night shift, and I gladly accepted. The foreman was very nice, too. He was from Yugoslavia.

After a few weeks, Art contacted me, asking whether I was interested in returning to my old position. He offered me an incentive of an additional ten cents per hour more than what I was currently making. I decided to go for it. Even though I liked my new job, I didn't enjoy working the night shift. Those hours were hard to get used to, and my body never fully made the adjustment. With Art's new offer, I was now making two dollars and eighty cents per hour. But even sweeter was that I was constantly working overtime.

Kristina and I had continued to correspond ever since I had arrived in California. But she had now sent me a letter that was quite shocking. She wanted money for an abortion. I was really taken aback by her request. Stunned, I decided not to respond because I didn't know what to say. Equally surprising was that she never wrote to me again.

Now that I seemed more settled, Tuli and Jolán advised me to consider finding my own place. They felt that because Irén had her own family, she needed her privacy. Jolán and Aron helped me find an apartment. They found me a furnished, one-bedroom duplex for eighty-five dollars per month that was located on Redondo Boulevard and Pickford Street. I had to figure out where I would spend dinnertime. Fortunately, I found a Hungarian restaurant where I ate at least four to five times each week.

THE COMET AND
A CHRISTMAS WEDDING

DURING 1960, I continued working and writing letters to Jessica. In one letter, I told her that the United States was a beautiful, excellent country, a great place for young people, and a land of opportunity. I added, however, that, even though America was great, I was still considering traveling throughout Asia, hoping to land a job in Japan.

In the meantime, my Pontiac broke down. It had run out of motor oil. I was forced to either rebuild the motor or purchase another car. Tuli suggested I rebuild the engine. It would have cost me two hundred and fifty dollars to rebuild. I opted to purchase a new car. Tuli and I went to a dealership. I bought the very first Mercury Comet ever made. It was a black beauty, which cost me a whopping two thousand four hundred dollars.

Jessica wrote back to me, saying she had an aunt living in Los Angeles. She told me to go visit her Auntie Rae and provided me with her address. One evening, I did what Jessica had suggested and went to visit her aunt. Rae had a good-looking family. I met her husband, Alf, and daughter, Brenda. Brenda was also British-born and had married an American soldier named Mike while living in England. Brenda and Mike also had a son born in England, named Neil, and an American-born son, Steven. After Brenda and her family moved to America, Rae and Alf had followed. We spent two hours chatting. Rae boasted about Jessica, saying she spoke beautifully and was a great cook. When she encouraged me to marry Jessica, I was surprised by her boldness. All in all, the visit was positive. I felt that Rae and her family approved of and liked me.

Shortly thereafter, Jessica sent me another letter telling me of her plans to come and visit America. She told me that her father was very ill and that her mother was encouraging her visit to America to try to start a new life.

Jessica arrived on October 25, 1960, and I was there to pick her up from the airport. I approached her and kissed her hand, and then we left in my new, jet-black Comet.

As we headed back to Los Angeles on the freeway, we both smelled something burning. I decided to exit the freeway at Slauson Avenue and go to a gas station. The mechanic at the gas station found that the car had a gas leak. I didn't want to drive it and cause any additional damage. The car was still under warranty and needed to be sent back to the dealer for the necessary repairs. I asked Jessica to call Tuli to pick us up. Jessica didn't know how to dial the phone, so the mechanic dialed the number for her. After speaking to him, Tuli came to pick us up in his car. He dropped Jessica off at Rae's place and took me back to my apartment.

Meanwhile, the Comet went back to the dealer for repairs. A few days later, after the car was fixed, I was able to visit Jessica. I decided it was time to introduce her to my family.

Our first visit was with Irén. Irén told Jessica that she had beautiful hands, legs, and feet. Then, we went to Jolán's where Jessica told me she felt like she was in a museum. Jolán kept her house in perfect order and in immaculately clean condition. Finally, I took her to Tuli's home. Esther invited Jessica to spend a couple nights at their home. Jessica felt most comfortable with Esther. They seemed to share the same tastes in style.

Jessica was living with her Aunt Rae, but the arrangements weren't working out as she had hoped. In exchange for a family to stay with and a place to live, Jessica was responsible for full-time baby-sitting, cooking, and cleaning. Jessica wanted different arrangements. I helped her escape by taking her to LACD. I gave her the option to date other men. She didn't find anyone who met her criteria.

In the meantime, my family was happy that I had a nice Jewish girlfriend. I was glad my family approved. How could they not?

Jessica was beautiful, was an extrovert, and could speak well. She tried hard to understand me because of my accent and language barrier. I also considered the fact that she had sacrificed her life and family in England to visit me in America.

Jolán decided to host a party for the entire family so Jessica could meet everyone under one roof. Out of respect for Jessica, Jolán served a British-style meal. They also invited her Aunt Rae and Uncle Alf. I felt that the dinner party was a setup. The issue of marriage arose, and before Jessica or I could say anything, the family was making wedding plans. They wanted us to wed in April, but the majority of the family felt that April wasn't appropriate because the Passover month occurred at the same time. Tuli and Esther thought differently. They said they could see no difference whether we wed immediately or later but suggested that we wed before the year's end for tax purposes. We decided to wed on Christmas Day at Hartman's Restaurant in the Fairfax district. Although everything happened so quickly and was out of my control, I agreed. I was afraid to lose Jessica.

Jolán, Esther, Irén, and Rae decided to give a wedding shower for Jessica. The costs were to be divided evenly among the hostesses. As the plans progressed, one of the hostesses complained about the cost, so Jessica paid for that hostess's portion. Overall, the wedding shower was beautiful, and Jessica received an abundance of gifts. In fact, she received so many gifts that they couldn't all fit into one car!

I began searching for another apartment. I had acquired a roommate along the way and didn't feel I should kick him out. I also felt that a change would do me good. By the first of December, I found another place. When I informed Art that I was moving and getting married, he was so happy that he gave me another raise, making my pay a flat three dollars per hour.

On December 18, Jessica and I went down to city hall to pick up our marriage certificate. After going to city hall, I told Jessica we would need to purchase protection for sexual intercourse because we

Our wedding photo with my side of the family. Back row, left to right: Mickey, Tuli, Esther, Sam, Irene, Jessica, me, Jolán, Aron, and Harry. In the front row, from left to right, are Harvey, Arthur, and Manny.

Off to the honeymoon.

were going to wait to have a family. Jessica didn't understand what I was talking about because she was still a virgin.

We stopped at the Thrifty Drug Store and I explained to Jessica what she needed to ask for at the pharmacy. As I had told her to, she went in and asked for a French Letter, a common British slang word for a condom, from the pharmacist. Being American and unfamiliar with the term, the pharmacist suggested she go to the post office. Jessica then had to explain in detail what she wanted. Eventually the pharmacist understood and told her that what she needed was a condom. Embarrassed and frustrated with the language barrier, she left.

And then she caught on. She told me we would wait until the rabbi married us and made it official. I told her that, according to American law, we were legally married, and that was good enough. But she insisted that our marriage wasn't proper unless we were married under Jewish law.

A week later, on December 25, 1960, Christmas Day, we were married at Hartman's. The rabbi signed our marriage certificate, and it was finally official. Thirty-five family members showed up for the occasion. It was a beautiful wedding.

Immediately after the wedding, we planned to drive to Las Vegas, Nevada. Instead, we went to the Sands Hotel in Brentwood to spend the night because I had been drinking heavily at the wedding. The following morning, we left for Las Vegas where we honeymooned at the Stardust Hotel. It was a brand-new hotel and very beautiful. Even so, Jessica felt lonely and upset because she was too young to gamble. She sat around feeling sorry for herself. In addition, Jessica expected us to try and create a baby immediately. I told her we had to wait. That statement perpetuated her crying, but I insisted that it was best to have a proper home before having a baby. We stayed in Las Vegas for one week. I lost approximately forty dollars. Out of all the games in Vegas, my favorite game was Keno through which I recovered the majority of the money I had initially lost.

CHAPTER 24 (1960–1961)

JESSICA GETS A JOB

ABOUT A week or so after our honeymoon, on a Sunday, Jessica awoke abruptly from a nap. She had dreamed that she saw her father smiling at her from the ceiling, and it made her nervous. I told her not to worry so much. Later that afternoon, we received a telegram that Jessica's father, Jacob Rapaport, had died from a brain tumor. Jessica was upset because she had not been able to be at her father's bedside when he passed away.

On Monday, I went back to my daily routine but, now, with Jessica as the housewife. When I came home from my first day back to work, Jessica had prepared me two pieces of chicken and a sack of potatoes. I couldn't believe she had cooked a whole sack of potatoes. She told me the practice was customary in her country. It was unacceptable by my standards, and I made that clear to her. I decided that Jessica would need to learn how to cook Hungarian style.

The next day, I took her to the Hungarian restaurant that I frequented. Jessica really loved the food and thought it rated as number one. Of course, this reaction pleased me.

After a few trips to the restaurant, Jessica decided she wanted to learn how to cook Hungarian food. Maria, the chef, really liked Jessica. Maria told Jessica that the restaurant never shared or gave out its recipes. However, she would allow Jessica to observe. Jessica picked up the recipes very quickly and naturally. She also bought a Hungarian cookbook. I was satisfied.

By March 1961, Jessica had become restless staying at home. She decided to look for a job. She found an advertisement in the newspaper looking for an expert on the Boroughs machine for Union Bank, located in downtown, Los Angeles. Jessica decided to respond to the ad, and she went the very next morning for an interview. They told her they couldn't accept a deaf person. Jessica told the manager she had two years experience with the Boroughs machine in England. She also presented a letter from her former employer in England.

The manager decided to give her a battery of tests to see her competency level and performance ability. She took the exams, and then they told her to come back in the afternoon for the results. It was a bit of a way home without transportation, so she decided to go out for lunch to bide the time.

When she returned, she thought she had the job because everyone was smiling at her. They told her she had passed the tests with one hundred percent accuracy. However, they could not hire her because she was deaf. Jessica told them that she didn't appreciate them playing dirty tricks on her and that she felt they had wasted her time by giving her all the tests.

When Jessica arrived home, she told me she felt she should go back to England. I urged her to calm down and reminded her that she was going through a lot of emotional changes—a new life, a new country, a new husband, the death of her father.

Later that evening, Tuli came to the house wanting to speak with Jessica. He told her that he had received a call from the Union Bank manager. The manager told Tuli that they were interested in Jessica, that she was hired, and that she should report to work first thing in the morning. We never found out the reason for their decision change, but we didn't really care. Jessica was happy that she could stay busy and be productive.

For entertainment, we continued going to LACD and to the Hebrew Association for the Deaf, or HAD, also located in downtown Los Angeles. Jessica played cards at HAD and socialized at both clubs. Jessica was a great card player. She always won.

After a while, Jessica became resistant to going to LACD. Many of the friends there greeted one another by kissing on the lips. Jessica was uncomfortable with that behavior and felt it was unnecessary. As a result, we made fewer and fewer trips to the club. I had to change my behavior to make our marriage work. It wasn't easy. Although we didn't frequent LACD as often for entertainment, I continued to play chess there weekly, maintaining my status as the champion of the deaf players in Los Angeles.

Other conflicts we faced stemmed from differences between our families' religious and cultural backgrounds as well as our languages and our communication styles. Jessica was proud to openly identify herself as a Jew. I wanted my Jewish heritage to be a secret. It bothered me when she wore the Star of David. I was concerned that people would mock her or throw stones at her. When Jessica first arrived from England, we had to rely on body language. My English was not perfect, and she did not know Hungarian. Often, she did not understand my intentions. My attempts to translate Hungarian to English often produced a different meaning from what I had in mind. I couldn't totally rely on the translations in the dictionaries either. I found myself regularly saying, "No. That is not what I meant." What was especially difficult was that Jessica was ashamed to use sign language publicly. As soon as I'd start signing, Jessica would say, "People are looking at you." And I'd respond, "So what. I am deaf and I'm proud of it. Forget those people." Years would go by before Jessica accepted signing in public.

Jessica continued pushing for a family. But I insisted that we own a home first. We decided that she would continue working until she got pregnant.

Overall, Jessica enjoyed her job. She had only one negative, though innocent, experience for which she was almost reprimanded. She had asked a coworker for a rubber. The coworker was offended by her request. Later, the manager summoned Jessica into his office and told her that she shouldn't ask other coworkers for condoms. Jessica was shocked that he said the word condoms. She defended herself and told the manager she had asked for a rubber, not a condom. She described what she needed. Luckily, the manager caught on to Jessica's request. He told her that, in America, a rubber is also known as a condom. What Jessica needed was an eraser. Once again, language had gotten in the way. Once again, and naturally, Jessica was embarrassed.

CHAPTER **25** (1962–1963)

JANUARY 18—SPIRITUAL FATE

TEN MONTHS later, we bought a house located at 8842 Horner Street, just off Robertson Boulevard in west Los Angeles. It was a Spanish-style home with two bedrooms, one bathroom, a large living room and kitchen, and a detached garage. It was a great starter home.

We had no furniture, but I gave Jessica the go-ahead to get pregnant. We tried for several months and failed. Jessica was frustrated. She went to the doctor complaining. He decided to run some blood tests. He found that she had an underactive thyroid and prescribed thyroid medication. Shortly thereafter, Jessica was pregnant. Her due date was December 25. I wanted a Christmas or New Year's baby. A Christmas baby would provide tax savings, and a New Year's baby would provide a cost-free delivery.

Five months later, Jessica's brother, Keith, came from England. By November 1962, Jessica's mother, Fanny, and sister, Deborah, came from England together. They all moved in with us, and Jessica quit her job. Jessica was happy that her family had come to America. She appeared calmer. She wanted her mother's help when the baby arrived. As it turned out, Jessica's pregnancy had complications. She suffered from high blood pressure and toxemia. So having her mother there was a blessing.

Jessica's family was always around, so I didn't feel guilty leaving her every evening to play chess. At this point, I played at the Herman Steiner Chess Club on Cashio and Robertson Boulevard because the LACD chess team had ceased to exist. One evening near midnight, Jessica appeared at the club in her pajamas, claiming that she was worried about me. I couldn't believe she'd check up on me in her pajamas.

December 25, our anniversary, came and went without a baby. Jessica was concerned because she was constantly having labor pains. Her doctor kept insisting that the baby wasn't ready to come out. As the pregnancy extended, the tension was reflected in our daily arguments about what to name our child.

I had just arrived home from work on January 17, 1963, when Fanny announced that Jessica was in mild labor and not to worry. But we were all worried because we had been able to see the shape of the baby's spine jutting out of Jessica's abdomen for nearly one week. However, Fanny calmly fed me a wholesome dinner, and I decided to go and play chess.

I returned home at seven thirty in the evening, and Fanny told me that Jessica was in hard labor. We rushed her to Cedars of Lebanon Hospital on Fountain Avenue in Hollywood. The labor went on and on. Jessica was not progressing. Fanny suggested that we go home and get some rest, assuring me that the hospital would call her when Jessica was ready to deliver. I agreed. I had to prepare myself for work the following morning anyway.

The next morning came, and I went to check on Jessica at the hospital—still no baby. So I went to work. Concentrating on work was difficult. As soon as the day ended, I rushed over to the hospital. Fanny was already there. Irén's husband, Sam, had dropped her off earlier because the hospital had called for her to go right away.

By six o'clock, the doctor decided that Jessica could not have a natural birth and would require a cesarean section. Up to this point, her doctor had been against the cesarean procedure. But he finally concluded that Jessica's pelvis was too narrow. I felt bad for Jessica because she had suffered for so many hours in hard labor.

The hospital staff wheeled her into the room just after seven o'clock to prepare her for surgery. I waited along with everyone else, pacing the hallways and wearing out the linoleum floor. Just past eight o'clock, the nurse came out and told me I had a daughter, born at one minute past eight. She told me that I would have to visit the intensive care unit because my daughter was extremely jaundiced.

I headed over to intensive care to see my daughter. On the way, I could see that Fanny and Jolán were waiting. When I arrived, the nurse had just finished bathing, weighing, and measuring my daughter. She weighed a hefty eight pounds, six-and-a-half ounces and was twenty-one inches long.

The next day, the family argued over what to name my daughter. Fanny told me that they wanted my daughter to be named Helen, which was the nickname for my mother Ilona. They wanted my daughter to have that name because she was the first girl in the family to be born in America. Jessica was adamant to pick another name. Fanny also suggested the name Eleanor, after Eleanor Roosevelt. She told me that I could use the name Helen as a nickname for Eleanor. We all settled on that name.

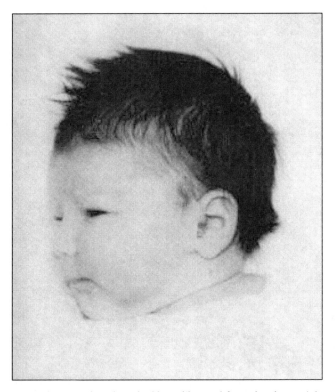

On January 18, the same date that I had been liberated from the ghetto eighteen years before, my daughter Eleanor came into this world.

That night when I returned home, I lay in bed thinking about all that had happened that day. Then it dawned on me. It was January 18—the very same date I had been liberated from the ghetto and given a second chance at life. I cried myself to sleep that night thinking about the irony of my life, my fate, and my destiny.

ENDNOTES

FOREWORD

1. Histories have been published for each school except the one at Budapest. Of the three, only the history of the London school appears in English: David Jackson, ed., *The History of the Residential School for Jewish Deaf Children* (London: Reunion of the Jewish Deaf School Committee, 1992). Appearing only in German language editions are (a) the history of the Vienna school, Walter Schott, *Das allgemeine österreichische isrealitische Taubstummen-Institut in Wien, 1844–1926* (Wien: Böhlau Verlag, 1995), and (b) the history for the Berlin, school, *"Öffne deine Hand für die Stummen": Die Geschichte der Israelitischen Taubstummen-Anstalt Berlin-Weissensee, 1873 bis 1942* (Berlin: Transit, 1993).

2. Dezső Kanizsai, ed., and Michael Mayer, trans., *1943–44 Yearbook* (Budapest: Jewish Deaf-Mute National Institute and Sir Ignaz Welselman and Zsofia Neushloss Educational Institute for the Blind, 1944).

3. David Cesarani, ed., *Genocide and Rescue, The Holocaust in Hungary, 1944* (Oxford: Berg, 1997), 5.

4. There many excellent histories of the Hungarian Holocaust. A respected historian of Hungary is one of the editors of a recently published history: Randolph L. Braham and Scott Miller, eds., *The Nazis' Last Victims, The Holocaust in Hungary* (Detroit: Wayne State University, 1998).

5. This meeting with the German military and Kanizsai's reaction is described in Otto Roboz, "The Red Cross Home of the Jewish Orphanage for Boys in Budapest," in *The Tragedy of Hungarian Jewry: Essays, Documents, Depositions* ed. Randolph L. Braham (New York: Columbia University Press, 1986), 295–96.

CHAPTER 2

1. Yehuda Bauer, *The Holocaust in Historical Perspective* (Seattle: University of Washington Press, 1978), 30–49.

2. Horst Biesold, *Crying Hands: Eugenics and Deaf People in Nazi Germany* (Washington, D.C.: Gallaudet University Press, 1999).

3. Raymond Hill, *Nations in Transition: Hungary* (New York: Facts on File, 1997), 21–46.

4. Biesold, *Crying Hands.*

5. James M. Glass, *Life Unworthy of Life* (New York: Harper Collins, 1997), 23–46.

6. Hill, *Nations in Transition*, 41.

7. Raul Hilberg, *The Destruction of the European Jews: Volume Two* (New York: Holmes and Meier, 1985), 799, 801.

8. Hill, *Nations in Transition*, 21–46.

9. John Weiss, *Ideology of Death: Why the Holocaust Happened in Germany* (Chicago: Ivan R. Dee, 1997), 317–41; Glass, *Life Unworthy of Life*, 47–65.

Chapter 3

1. Raymond Hill, *Nations in Transition: Hungary* (New York: Facts on File, 1997), 21–46.

2. Ibid.

Chapter 4

1. Leni Yahil, *The Holocaust: The Fate of European Jewry* (New York: Oxford University Press, 1990), 312–16.

2. Ibid, 305, 310–12, 332.

Chapter 5

1. Leni Yahil, *The Holocaust: The Fate of European Jewry* (New York: Oxford University Press, 1990), 519.

2. Raul Hilberg, *The Destruction of the European Jews: Volume Two* (New York: Holmes and Meier, 1985), 797; Raymond Hill, *Nations in Transition: Hungary* (New York: Facts on File, 1997), 44.

Chapter 6

1. Leni Yahil, *The Holocaust: The Fate of European Jewry* (New York: Oxford University Press, 1990), 505.

2. Raul Hilberg, *The Destruction of the European Jews: Volume Two* (New York: Holmes and Meier, 1985), 823, 843–44.

3. John Weiss, *Ideology of Death: Why the Holocaust Happened in Germany* (Chicago: Ivan R. Dee 1997), 341; Hilberg, *The Destruction of the European Jews: Volume Two*, 850.

4. Hilberg, *The Destruction of the European Jews: Volume Two*, 1138.

5. Danny Smith, *Wallenberg: Lost Hero* (Springfield, Illinois: Templegate, 1986).

Chapter 7

1. Raymond Hill, *Nations in Transition: Hungary* (New York: Facts on File, 1997), 45.

2. Leni Yahil, *The Holocaust: The Fate of European Jewry* (New York: Oxford University Press, 1990), 515.

3. Raul Hilberg, *The Destruction of the European Jews: Volume Two* (New York: Holmes and Meier, 1985), 856–58.

4. Yahil, *The Holocaust*, 457–98.

CHAPTER 8

1. Danny Smith, *Wallenberg: Lost Hero* (Springfield, Illinois: Templegate, 1986), 104–16.

CHAPTER 9

1. Jean-Claude Favez, *The Red Cross and the Holocaust* (United Kingdom: Cambridge University Press, 1999).

2. Raul Hilberg, *The Destruction of the European Jews: Volume Three* (New York: Holmes and Meier, 1985), 1140.

CHAPTER 10

1. In Hungary, what Americans refer to as the Torah is referred to as the Bible.

2. December 6 is St. Nicholas Day, which is celebrated in Hungarian Catholic culture.

EPILOGUE

MY LIFE has not been easy, but it has brought me rewards nonetheless. I went through powerful experiences as a boy. Being not only Jewish but also deaf often made them even harder. Yet all of the hardships I endured shaped me into who I am today—a family man who is open-minded, who understands the importance of freedom, and who appreciates the ability to travel.

My greatest pleasure in life is my family. Jessica and I have three daughters—Eleanor, Hannah, and Karen—and now they all have families of their own. After ten years of marriage, Jessica realized that she could live in both the hearing world and the deaf world. Ever since, we have signed together in public. We have had our ups and downs, but they come with marriage. Whether a situation is bad or good, we have learned to work through it and accept it.

I have never felt sorry for myself. I grew up adaptable, versatile, and hardy, like a wildflower. My brothers and sisters split up in different directions without me, so I planted myself wherever I could. Fate, history, Hitler and his evil, and politics created a gap between my family and me that has never fully closed, but in our hearts, we are family. Eventually, all of my brothers and sisters, except Magda, moved to the Los Angeles area. Magda has stayed in Israel. All of my siblings, except Lenke, are still living, and we have given one another many nieces and nephews.

I don't practice Judaism anymore. Too many things have happened in my life that made me question the existence of God. I do believe in karma and in fate. My fate was to be deaf, but being deaf saved my life. If I had been hearing, I would not have survived the war. I would have been sent to Auschwitz along with the other members of my family. Instead, I was sent to Budapest where, with luck and determination, I stayed alive.

181

CPSIA information can be obtained
at www.ICGtesting.com
Printed in the USA
FFOW03n1517101217
43941213-43018FF